Like Moonlight at Low Tide

NICOLE QUIGLEY

BLINK

Like Moonlight at Low Tide

This title is also available as a Blink ebook. Visit www.zondervan.com/ebooks.

Requests for information should be addressed to:

Blink, *5300 Patterson Ave SE, Grand Rapids, Michigan 49530*

ISBN 978-0-310-72360-8

Ms. Bowie's description of the Milky Way is paraphrased from Louis Giglio's "Indescribable" talk, available on YouTube (http://www.youtube.com/watch?v=BUtuEOAoWD8&feature=related) and via DVD.

Cover design: Kris Nelson
Cover photography: plainpicture/Jasmin Sander
Interior design and composition: Greg Johnson/Textbook Perfect and Ben Fetterley

Printed in the United States of America

13 14 15 16 17 18 19 /DCI/ 20 19 18 17 16 15 14 13 12 11 10 9 8 7 6 5 4 3 2

Like Moonlight at Low Tide

For my parents,
John and Ellen Quigley,
who taught me to dream.

In memory of
Christopher M. "Chuck" Truman
(1976–1992)

Chapter 1

People never ask me the right question when they ask me what happened the beginning of my senior year. They always ask what his last words were. They figure he would have had great ones, the kind that would haunt a girl and echo off of empty lockers long after graduation. They wait breathlessly for me to describe the moment he jumped off the boat and into the glass-topped Gulf, cutting the ribbon of moonlight on the surface with the white of his arms.

"Surely he was trying to kill himself," they'd say. "Why else would he leap into the water without the hope of rescue?"

And so I tell them what they earnestly hope to hear. How I searched desperately for the bob of his head in the water. How I jumped in myself, swimming fifteen feet until I felt the absence of the boat behind me, the vessel leaning away from the edge of the bay and into the dark, magnetic waters of the deep. They want to hear how hard it was to make my way back to the boat, and how, by then, the storm was beginning to unleash its rage. They want to hear how I scoured the cabinets for a radio and failed. How I searched for a flare gun but found no rescue.

And when I tell them of all of these things, they never ask—and I never mention—that I did all of them in complete silence.

The truth is, he said nothing before he jumped. And I never called his name, not once. I knew that he had plunged into that water so that he could not be found.

When the sheriff pulled his boat next to mine, he spoke the first words I had heard in hours. He lifted me from beneath the captain's console, where I had waited with my knees tucked under my chin. That was the evening Hurricane Paul swept through our state.

This story is not about suicide. But you should know that when I was seventeen, the only boy who ever called me by my full name took his own life. It was the first time I ever saw a mistake that was permanent, that couldn't be undone with whiteout or atoned for with an after-school detention. Nothing else I do for the rest of my life will ever be able to change this fact.

This story is actually about three boys. One who loved me. One who couldn't. And one who didn't know how.

My name is Melissa Keiser, and I was raised on Anna Maria Island, Florida.

The best description of the place I can provide you is a temperature: eighty degrees. It is not always eighty degrees on the island, but the humidity looming off the white foam of the Gulf of Mexico combined with the faint, sickly sweet emission from the orange juice factory always seems to make the place feel like it's been wrapped in a warm blanket, just soft enough to make you feel safe or sleepy, but always feel slow if you tried to move too much within its folds. In truth, it is the most beautiful beach town I have ever seen. And then the breeze comes and reality finds you hiding behind a sand dune.

The Anna Maria I'm writing of is not the same island that you would see if you went online and searched the images posted by Yankee tourists and gray-haired Canadians. Those visitors love the island as much as anyone who has never suffered here can. They post pictures of things like starfish and sandcastles and pelicans at sunset. They marvel at the brightly colored flowers that seem to grow from the ditches like weeds, and the waist-high herons, and the restaurants grilling grouper underneath tin-roofed sun decks. This is, after all, a place overflowing with such abundant beauty that its residents actually chased off native, jewel-colored peacocks to the neighboring cities because it deemed them a nuisance. Only an island sure of its place among beach towns could afford to do such a thing without regret.

But pictures of these things don't show what life was like for me or for the others who walked these streets that year. To the tourists, we are points of curiosity. They wonder what it would be like to raise their children in a place where the speed limit is twenty-five and the town shuts down for the high school football game. And we oblige to tell them and show them how to pick up crabs with their bare hands. This is what happens when you're surrounded by people who visit for two weeks at a time, intent on happiness, always reminding us of how wonderful the island is compared to where they live, because where they live is lucky to have a city park and a tree that has kept its leaves. But when the conversation ends, we never make it into their pictures.

In the time since I was a child, those tourists have slowly razed the neighborhoods of my youth, house by house, in order to build pink, tall homes in their place that people like my family could never afford to rent. But that was never the point. Now, their new winter domains sit empty six months out of the year, while locals move to the concrete mainland in search of cheaper rent. It is an odd thing, to love these visitors and to depend on them for supper, while at the same time knowing the more who come will mean less room for us.

But I am writing of the island not pictured on Google, the one that still harbors the necessary number of the working class who have found a way to make a home on a seven-mile stretch of paradise without the rich folks noticing.

• • • • •

When my mother moved us back in the winter of my junior year after spending three years up north, it felt like a flood was coming and I had forgotten how to swim.

"When are you coming home?" I regretted my tone instantly because I knew exactly what it was going to get me.

"It's none of your business," Denise shouted into the phone to mask the sound of the band starting up in the background. "I left ten dollars on the kitchen table. Go to the store and buy some subs for you and your sister." My mother was certain that ten dollars could solve most of my complaints, whatever they were. She never used the same tactic with Robby. My older brother never had to babysit, and he was never home long enough for us to consider that he would.

"I don't want to have to be here all night, Mom."

"You don't have a choice, Missy. I gotta go." The band started its rowdy thump in the background as the phone clicked off. Maybe tips at the restaurant would be good tonight.

I turned to my sister in resignation. "It's you and me again, Crystal. Put on your shoes. We're going to get some dinner."

She struggled with the strap of her sandal until I squatted down and gently brushed her hands away. These things were always easier when I fixed them myself. She was too small to help with much of anything, and I was certain she wouldn't be growing anytime soon. She hadn't grown in a year. This would be alarming to a doctor, if we could afford one, considering she was only seven.

"Wrong way," I said, quietly. I tugged her hand in the other direction so we would walk down Gulf Drive instead of our neighborhood road, where Tanya Maldonado would have surely spotted me from inside her climate-controlled home. I hadn't seen Tanya since middle school, since before my mother made us chase her boyfriend Doug to the gray hills of Pennsylvania.

And even though I had been gone for three years, I knew she would be waiting for me as if I hadn't missed a day. In middle school, she had found everything I did to be endlessly fascinating.

If I fixed my hair a different way, it gave her entertainment for a week.

"Do you think you look pretty with that new haircut?" she'd ask with narrowed eyes.

If I had managed to get a new outfit, she'd demand to know all of the details.

"Is that shirt new? I've never seen one like that before ... It's almost like a boy's shirt, isn't it?"

I could avoid her attention many days by taking an extra long time in the bathroom stall, waiting for the warning bell to sound so I could rush off to class without having to face her.

This worked for several weeks until almost the end of seventh grade. I sat on the toilet and held my breath when she entered with all of her friends, setting up a virtual beauty parlor in front of the age-spotted mirror. Between the pops and clicks of makeup bottles, I heard her give her army its marching orders.

"Ask *Messy* if she likes Sam King. She totally does. As if he would ever be seen with her!" I could hear the group smacking their lips to blend the fresh applications of glitter lip gloss. "I have a hard time even sitting next to her in class. I'm afraid she has bugs that will jump off onto me or something."

The girls giggled with excitement as if they had just decided on a new dance routine and headed out with a renewed sense of purpose. Tanya Maldonado had given them a job to do, and by the end of the day all five of them would test me to see if the unthinkable rumor was true. Had Melissa "Messy" Keiser actually dared to like one of the school's star athletes?

The truth was that I had never told a soul I had a crush on Sam King. But in the cafeteria at lunch, Tanya had the perfect view of everything I had hoped to hide. She sat at the center table of the center of popular kids, where she practically ruled the entire middle school from the throne of our social universe.

When Sam passed by my seat to get near her, a blotch of pink brushed across my cheeks, and I saw Tanya zero in on it like a sharp shooter. It was all the confirmation she needed, and she pounced at the opportunity. Within minutes, half of her table was glaring at me through the corners of their eyes and the other half was shaking with laughter. Their eyebrows were raised so high that their foreheads wrinkled in confusion, as if whatever thoughts were crossing their minds were unthinkable. As if they were looking at someone who was certifiably crazy.

Sam was in seventh grade, like us, but he already had friends in the ninth grade and the high school coaches already knew his name. He never made eye contact with me after the rumors began, but a gang of his friends rushed in to protect his reputation accordingly.

"You do know you're ugly, Messy?" said one in the hallway as I passed.

I pretended not to hear it. Just maybe, hopefully, I had heard wrong.

And then, in science, loud enough so I could hear from a few rows back, "She's a total dog."

This began the new way I was greeted every time I entered the class. The boys would bark like a pack of dogs when I walked into the room and chuckle when I passed by. It was not until the Ian Owens episode that the trouble stopped. The student council vice president turned around from the front row, looked at me, and grabbed the sides of his cheeks in horror as if he had just seen a ghost. The message was clear: I was a fright to see.

The teacher gave Ian a detention for the incident, and it seemed the barking lost its novelty. An event like that was hard to top. But by the end of the ordeal, I had been called ugly thirty school days in a row. By various people. Even by Mike Lewis when he passed me alone in the hallway and shoved my books hard into my chest, attacking where no one else was even there to see him do it. My family moved away several months afterward, just before the first semester of eighth grade came to a close. I got to finish middle school and start high school in a new town, where no one knew me as Messy, where no one knew me at all.

I tell you all of this so you will understand just what was at stake by the time I returned to the island just a few years later, over the winter break of my junior year. I was about to transfer back and face all of those same people again. I held out the hope that outright name-calling and barking was something that ended at the high school doors, but I knew there was no way that I could escape the stigma, the memory of what it meant to be Messy Keiser. The only good thing I looked forward to about returning home to Florida was the chance to swim again, any time of year, and already knowing that my old friend, Julie Peterson, was right where I had left her, seemingly immune to the scorn that came with being my best friend. I had one strategy to get me through my return to the island. Hide.

When Denise finally returned from work, it was past midnight, and I was pretending to be asleep in my bed with the radio set to low. I heard her keys hit the glass table and the door to Crystal's room open and shut briefly for a check-in. She walked past the locked door to my bedroom and on to her own, where I heard her release a dark giggle that followed the low, unmistakable rumble of a man I was sure I didn't know. I waited five minutes before I applied another coat of lip gloss, popped out the screen of my bedroom window, and lifted its heavy glass as high as it would go. We were lucky the rental house was big enough for all of us to have our own rooms, even if Robby's was just a converted glassed-in porch off the back.

I darted across the grass, crushing its fresh, stiff blades. I sprinted through the unfenced backyards of my neighbors' houses until I made it to the opposite street. The earth seemed to palpably rotate beneath me, an accomplice to my escape, if only for a while.

When I arrived at Julie's house five blocks away, I could hear the thump of music from the curb. A car and a truck were parked out front, but I knew neither belonged to Julie's family.

"I thought you were never going to get here!" Julie shook her head in disbelief at the sight of my hair in a bun at the top of my head. "I can't believe your mom makes you babysit on Saturday nights!"

"I have my swimsuit on underneath my clothes in case your parents let us go for a swim. Where are they, anyway? And whose cars are those?"

She pulled me through the front door and began to tug on her lower lip with a devious grin. "My parents are still out for the night."

I searched her expression. Tugging on her lower lip was Julie's giveaway. She hadn't revealed everything. "And?" I pressed.

"Well, follow me."

We rounded the living room and past the photos of her family on vacation. The wall was plastered with bejeweled, framed scenes of cruises and Jamaican timeshares and postcards from Mexico with images of her satisfied father and her bronzed, big-haired mother. They were a certain breed of Floridian, the kind who lived on an island and vacationed on islands. They knew what they liked, and there was no reason to waste time on what they didn't. I also remembered they were the type of parents who actually complained when their children didn't party enough. This must have been the reason Julie and I got along so well. We both understood why it was important to count your mother's drinks after five o' clock.

When we arrived on her back porch, two boys were playing with lighters, holding their palms over the open flames until one of them flinched from the pain. I froze in shock at the sight of them until

Julie nudged me from behind. I knew exactly who they were, and I took a seat in a white wicker chair, dreading the moment they would look up, which neither of them did for another two minutes.

Just beyond them I saw the demure frame of Julie's other best friend. "Hey, Leigh," I waved as she looked up from the orange flame shooting from Brett Smith's fingers. Leigh Doherty had grown out her long, wavy blonde hair since I had last seen her. And this, I decided, made her the most beautiful girl in the room.

"I didn't think you were hanging out tonight. Julie said you had to babysit." She talked as nonchalantly as if she was finishing a conversation from earlier in the day, although I hadn't actually seen her since I was thirteen.

"Yeah, well, my mom had to work a double so I just got off."

"Sucks." Leigh shrugged. "You should have been out at the docks earlier. Everyone was there. Welcome back, by the way."

"Hey," Brett said. He flipped the lid of his lighter shut and turned to me for the first time. "I remember you."

"Hey." I answered. I remembered him too. He was friends with Ian Owens and Mike Lewis, and one of the outliers of the clan of kids who had tortured me. This was how it went when the world around me was divided into two camps. Every guy I knew was part of the group that couldn't stand me or part of the group that didn't know me. And now Leigh had apparently crossed enemy lines to date one of the former.

Brett squinted his eyebrows together as if searching his memory. "Didn't they used to call you Messy?" He smirked as if he was proud of himself for remembering something so far in the past, something that was surely nothing more to him than seventh-grade entertainment.

"Shut up," Julie interrupted. "Her name's Missy."

"I remember you now, *Messy*." He grinned in defiance until Julie threw a Frisbee at his head. "Just kidding."

"*Missy* just moved back from Pennsylvania."

"That's cool," Brett answered. He nodded his head slightly and slumped back into his chair, seemingly already bored with the topic.

"And what did they used to call *you* in the seventh grade?" Julie eyed him with a wry smile.

"The man. The king. Most eligible. You can take your pick."

"Eligible?" Leigh raised her eyebrows until Brett burrowed his head into her neck as if to ask forgiveness.

Julie rolled her eyes. "No one calls her Messy anymore. That was seventh grade, and we're in high school now, old man."

"Yeah. Well, she does look different." He moved his eyes over my body as if examining me for a science fair.

I looked to the floor, unsure what he meant by the comment and afraid to let him see me flinch in case it wasn't good.

"I'm bored. I'm going inside to watch TV," Leigh said with a dramatic sigh. She pulled her blonde waves to the side of one shoulder and rose with her chest pushed out. Brett followed her as if on a leash until the two disappeared into an empty room deep inside the house.

"Don't mind him. He didn't have his meds today."

I shrugged. Julie was trying to make up for Brett's rudeness, but I was already sorry I came.

"Whatever." She shook her head and crossed her legs to the other side as if to create a fresh start. "You remember JP, right?"

The only boy left in the room tucked the sun-tipped strands of his shaggy hair behind his ears and peered back with a vacant smile. He held my eyes for a few seconds, nodded, and turned his attention back to Julie. I wondered if she had noticed he was interested in her. The silence that had built up between them was heavy enough to collapse the porch.

I remembered JP well, and how he always came across cooler than the other guys due to the fact that he rarely spoke. And since his mind always seemed to be somewhere else, the girls who swarmed around him had the opportunity to believe he was quiet because he was thinking about them, pining for them in reciprocal obsession.

When we began middle school, the county bused everyone from Anna Maria over two bridges to Bradenton on the mainland, where we mixed with kids who lived in neighborhoods with names that sounded like distant seas and rules that prohibited ghastly things like overgrown shrubbery and outside laundry lines. We arrived at the intown school with sand pouring out of our backpacks, still fighting a cough from red tide. But the sound of us struggling from the toxic algae that sometimes attacked our coast only added to our sense of mystery—as if we lived under a pier and cooked our meals over bonfires. And when girls from the mainland got wind of the tan, surfer guy who was too cool to speak and who went by only two initials, they didn't have a hope at resisting him.

But JP's mind was more likely to be on the waves. I knew this because, when the bus would finally return us to the island every afternoon, we would all stop our chatter to watch his reaction as we drove by the public beach. If JP could get in just the right position on the left side of the bus, he could make out the lifeguard stand and the flag the guard had posted to mark the beach conditions. If that flag was any color other than green, his mouth would pop open in excitement, and he'd switch seats until he reached the front of the bus so he could be the first one down the steps and on to the street. A flag that wasn't green meant the surf was rough for swimmers, which meant it might be cresting enough to be worth his time to head to the shore, where the often placid Gulf of Mexico would release its power and offer him a ride. It was the only time he ever looked interested in what was happening around him. Until now.

Julie bit her lower lip to hide the blush that was sweeping across her cheeks. Suddenly, her long-lost best friend's return was not the most interesting thing to happen to her during winter break.

The only real friend I had on the island had just discovered she had a boyfriend. I tightened my stomach to discipline the feelings welling up in my gut. I would not be jealous, not of Julie. It was a good thing that she had found a boyfriend, and I was content to come along and pretend that I too was wanted, by association, by the broad-shouldered boys who drove trucks and who weren't afraid to surf in terrifying storms.

"I'm getting tired. See you tomorrow, y'all."

"So soon?" Her eyes didn't leave JP's boyish smile.

"Yeah, good night."

I had been gone for years, but Brett had made it clear that they all remembered me: the girl who went to school in the same outfits every day, the girl whose mother had never made it to a parent-teacher night. The empty feeling in my stomach returned as I thought of going back to school with those same kids. Despite the few inches I had grown, it was like I had never left, as if that awkward, thirteen-year-old girl I so hated would always return to cast her rejected shadow wherever I went. I wanted the year to be over before second semester had even begun. But high school doesn't come with an escape hatch.

When I was nearing home I tiptoed through my neighbors' backyards and stopped when I got to Mrs. Durham's house next door. There was one place I could always hide. I poked my finger through a hole in the screened door of her backyard lanai, untwisting the lock until the handle released and I could view the familiar sight of dolphin figurines and potted plants. Not much had changed in the years I had been away. My family had managed to return to the same old rental house where we used to live, and I could still predict the vacancy schedule of our block to a science. It was the off-season, so there were several weeks before Mrs. Durham and all of the other Michigan grandmothers would return to the island to make their homes for the winter. There inside her abandoned lanai, her dark, glistening pool was waiting for me. And just as I had expected, Mrs. Durham had kept the maintenance man coming and the solar panels charging, so this oasis would be waiting for her in perfect condition upon her return.

I cut the water slowly with my long arms and swam to the deep end, allowing myself to sink to the bottom in the quiet. Strands of my dark brown hair transformed into black ribbons, swirling above my head. There was freedom in the water, in the calm of it. I was alone, night swimming, making forbidden currents that enfolded every curve of my skin. In this place, no one had ever called me Messy, and my mother would never think to look for me.

I floated flat on my back and tried to convince myself that things could be different this time on the island. That just maybe I could learn to be happy in paradise. And all I needed was so simple and yet so far away that it could crush me. If I had to put a name to it ... If I had to boil it down to its simplest part ... If I was really being honest ... I needed to know that someone thought I was pretty. Just one boy to say I was beautiful. That would undo everything the others had ever said to me.

As my eyes grew heavy and I started to shiver from the night air, I forced myself out of the pool, collected my clothes, and let the water rain from the seams of my suit. I returned to my bedroom window, hair dripping, skin exhaling chlorine, and slipped inside to my bedroom, where the door was still locked from the inside. I was glad some things hadn't changed, and glad for Mrs. Durham's pool most of all.

Just as I lowered my blinds, a beam of light shot from Mrs. Durham's deserted winter house and shocked the inside of my bedroom with a white flood. It came from one of her bedrooms like a flash and turned off just as quickly. Someone was home next door. I dodged to the side of the wall and lowered my blinds with a crash. There was no more movement coming from her house, and I was left to fall asleep wondering how I could have missed her early return.

Chapter 2

Although I spotted Mrs. Durham's Buick at no less than three island strip malls over the next few days, the woman was nowhere to be seen. I had not caught her garage door open even once.

Apart from the few seconds of blinding light that had shot through my bedroom at two in the morning, there were no signs of life from the Durham home. On one occasion, I even baited Crystal into walking the aisles of the Sandy Dock hardware store, where I was certain I caught the backside of Mrs. Durham's blueish, permed hair through the storefront window, meandering amidst the paint aisle. Crystal returned from the store to meet me at my lookout perch with a report that there wasn't a single woman in the entire place.

"Crystal says you're stalking the old lady next door." My brother sat at the kitchen table with a towel over his head to catch the salt water.

"I am not. I'm just trying to figure out if she's home."

"Why would you even care?" Robby raised his eyebrows as if he had a right to interrogate me. He always seemed to know when I was trying to hide something. Though he was a year older than me, we had been in the same grade ever since he stayed back a year in elementary school. It was useless to try to do anything without him finding out.

"It's none of your business," I said. "Someone flipped a switch on in there the other night. It was like a spotlight. I'm just wondering if we got new neighbors is all."

"Okay, crazy. Well, quit dragging Crystal into your little detective work. You're going to give her issues."

Crystal sucked on her thumb and blinked slowly. She was far too old to be sucking her thumb, but the sight of her bright blue eyes looking between us ended the conversation. Crystal had never judged us, not a day in her life, and neither of us was going to give her cause.

"Whatever," I huffed.

"I know what you're up to," Robby taunted once Crystal left the room. "You're going pool hopping over there just like you used to do in middle school because it's the only heated pool in three blocks. But it doesn't matter what you think you saw. It could have been a car passing by for all you know. We have at least four more weeks until the snowbirds come back, and no one is home over there. That house is a tomb."

"I'm not sure is all. I just don't want to get caught."

"If you're gonna do it, then do it. Don't be such a pansy." He wobbled his head to show me it was a dare. He loved getting me unhinged. It was his favorite pastime after skim boarding.

I stood up from the table and pulled the towel off of his hair with a shove. "I'll do it if I want to do it."

"Fine, Missy. If you want, I'll go over there with you one night and show you no one's there."

"I'm not scared." My skin prickled at the lie. "Besides, I only go alone. You're not invited."

Robby must have known that offering to chaperone me would be the only thing to get me to go back to the house on my own. He always seemed to know what made people tick, which must have bored him, because he never made an effort to get to know anyone for too long. My big brother fit in exactly nowhere. He was too smart to be a total stoner and too apathetic to be popular. The result was that I got absolutely no social benefit for being a year younger than him. No hot friends knocking on my door. No upperclassman looking out for me. I couldn't follow in his footsteps because he left no prints. My only link to any sort of social life at high school was going to be my best friend Julie.

As winter break drew to a close, Julie had grown less available as her new romance with JP began to weave its way into every plan we attempted to make. The coy glances between them had exploded into a full-out official relationship in a matter of days. Within five days of the porch party, JP had asked Julie to go to prom, which we both thought was rather early in the relationship to raise. But anyone who had seen the way JP looked at her would understand. He was not going to give any other guy a moment of opportunity.

She owned the issue gracefully. "The only reason I have a date so soon is because I have been going to school here all along. You've been gone. When school starts back up, there are so many hot guys . . . You'll see."

Hot guys. I knew one would be there, in particular, but I hadn't seen him in three years. And I had no idea how Sam King would look now that he was a junior.

"Plus," Julie added. "Now that JP is my boyfriend, we can hang out with all of his friends. Some of them don't even go to school in Bradenton."

I was able to muster genuine happiness for her when we went to the mall to try on formal dresses. It was too early to buy one for prom, but it wasn't too early to dream about it. They were pink and happy and the sort of thing I had not been able to admit I ever wanted to wear until she handed me one in the dressing room. I slipped on the silky wonder and entertained, if only for a second, the idea that some boy from in town, a boy who had never barked at me in middle school, would ask me to go. But I could only live in my head so long.

• • • • •

That Monday was the first day of school, second semester of my junior year, and there was nothing close to a gorgeous, pink dress in my closet. I needed to find an outfit that made me look put-together and new and nothing like the girl they used to know in seventh grade, but I was lucky to scrape together a loose, navy blue top and a pair of skinny jeans.

If there was an advantage to having been gone these last few years, it was that all of my Pennsylvania clothes were new to the kids in Florida. I had a closet full of old jeans and tops that they had never seen me in, as if I had just ransacked the mall in a back-to-school shopping spree. Of course, most of the clothes were cold-weather sweaters that I wouldn't need anymore, but there was just enough usable stuff that they would have no way of knowing that the only school shopping I did for the new semester was for a new notebook. I checked my reflection in the hallway mirror to be sure the pants I wore were still making me look thin even after a bowl of cereal. I stood tall and sucked in my gut until I was satisfied that I had found a skinny posture I could maintain all day. If I had to face Tanya Maldonado and Ian Owens and the countless boys who would elbow each other at the sight of my face, I would at least do it looking my best. Denise had left Robby and me money for lunch on the kitchen table and was dragging her bare feet across the kitchen tile in search of coffee. It was one of those rare days when she had everything together.

"No big deal, guys," she said under her breath. "You know all these kids already. It's just been a few years."

"Right," I mumbled. That was exactly the problem.

Crystal spooned gobs of rainbow-colored cereal to her mouth and smiled widely in recognition of our big day.

"You excited for your first day of school on the island?"

"Of course she is," Denise answered for her. "She was always an island girl, anyway. Who needs those old Pennsylvania schools? Now you'll have a year-long tan, right, baby?"

Crystal nodded in agreement as Robby breezed past the table with his messenger bag slung over his shoulder.

"Robby, aren't you going to get your sister a ride?"

I froze, not wanting to look too eager.

"I would, but there's no room in Ricky's car. I'm the fourth rider. Sorry, Miss."

At the bus stop on Palm Drive I recognized the old faces from middle school, broader and more defined now. But they were the same kids I remembered, now covered in zits and with better-groomed hair.

We mumbled "hey" and acted too preoccupied with superior thoughts to engage in any further conversation. I tried not to bite my nails as I waited impatiently for the bus to arrive. It was then that I noticed the strange boy clothed in layers of dark cotton shirts and leaning against a palm tree by the sidewalk. He was too rugged to be hip, but something about him reminded me of JP, as if he would be more comfortable in his bodysuit at the beach than in dry clothes boarding a bus to leave the island. I wondered where in the neighborhood he lived.

He peered from under a mess of dark brown hair as if he was entirely unconcerned with the fact that Tanya Maldonado was making her way up the block in her long leggings and belted dress. I was certain the surfer must have been Canadian, because no red-blooded American boy I knew could have possibly looked so aloof when Tanya made her way down the street, her perfect figure clearing a pathway through the freshmen as she arrived with the cool stride of a girl who only dated college guys. I was shocked to see she was still riding the yellow wagon too, and in some way I imagined it took the edge off the severity of my own dilemma.

I looked down immediately, hoping to avoid eye contact. And when I flinched, looking up for a second in the vain hope that the bus was arriving, she exhaled loudly as her eyes stumbled upon me. A subtle, wicked pout slipped over her face until she stepped in front of Surfer Boy and mumbled, "Hey."

Nothing, it seemed, had changed.

I took a seat near the front of the bus, far away from the back row where I knew she'd be holding court. Surfer Boy did not sit in the back with her. Instead, he plopped on the vinyl seat across from me, right behind the bus driver like a freshman. I burned a hole through the corner of my eyes trying to see him, willing him to tell me his story. But he didn't. Instead he plugged his iPod into his ears, stared sharply ahead, and I set about my first days at school without any hope of distraction from the core mission of blending in and taking cover.

In classes where seats weren't assigned, I raced for the back. At lunch, I meandered around the salad bar until Julie arrived so I could walk with her to the safety of our table by the window, far from the popular booths where Tanya was sitting with impunity. The old dog pack was everywhere: in homeroom, in chemistry, in Algebra II. They did double takes when they saw me slouching in the back of class, the beginnings of the old name coming out of their mouths until they paused, inexplicably, and broke down into wide, mischievous grins.

In the evenings, when I plodded off the bus to head home, Surfer Boy was nowhere to be found. I would get off the bus alone and wonder if he was already inside his house somewhere on my street, spying on me through his kitchen window as I walked past unknowingly.

But that was just another daydream. Reality was a different matter.

There were new kids at high school, ones who didn't know me and who didn't know that *Missy* was not what they would likely be calling me in a few weeks' time, after the old crowd would find some excuse to broadcast who I really was. I dreaded the inevitable return of Messy so much that I cringed every time I heard someone call my real name, double checking whether I was hearing the *i* or the *e*. I resented my name. It would be better if they called me nothing at all.

During lunch at the end of the second week, my respite of invisibility came to an end. Tanya Maldonado looked over to my direction from the popular booths, made a face like she had just drunk sour milk, and laughed in unison with the three girls flanking each of her sides. Ian Owens had just barked like a dog.

If it weren't happening to me, I could admit that Ian's bark was remarkably spot-on for a terrier, which only made it funnier, which only made him do it more. It was YouTube worthy.

Julie forced out a smile and asked how Algebra II was going. I could see in her eyes the futile hope that I hadn't heard.

"Fine," I said.

"Oh, that's good." She tugged on her lip as if she was searching for a subject to get me talking.

But we were horrible at making small talk when we could both feel it was all happening over again. It would be only a matter of time before they found a way to remind the whole school who I really was. My hiatus off the island was too short to let them forget. I lifted my hand to my forehead to cover my face and pushed the remnants of a salad around my plate. If I could just avoid eye contact, maybe they'd stop before it got too loud.

"Hey, girls," JP mumbled as he flopped into a seat next to Julie.

"How's the popular table?" she asked, rolling her eyes.

"Whatever." He puckered his lips as if she owed him a kiss for the remark. Julie obliged.

I forgot about JP's ability to float between groups, and how he was one of *them*. Had been since sixth grade. Where was he when the barking started? Did he laugh? I coughed back tears. I would not cry in the lunchroom.

JP opened up a new carton of skim milk, and I fanned the hope that he had been in the cafeteria line when Ian began his impression. "So, Missy, how does it feel to be back? Everyone remembers you, that's for sure. They were just talking about you." He nodded toward the booths.

Julie and I looked at him, cross. Was he really saying that?

"They're all saying how different you look now. Especially Sam King."

The breath rushed from my lungs so fast that I didn't have time to recover my face. Julie and I exchanged glances.

"Why do you look like you just saw a ghost?" JP asked. He grinned impishly and stuffed some of our fries into his mouth.

"She doesn't," Julie hissed.

"Sam King?" I repeated flatly. "I haven't seen him since middle school."

"Well ..." JP pointed. "He's right there sitting with Tanya and everybody else. Some things haven't changed."

I mustered the courage to look up and study the faces around Tanya's booth. Every guy looked the same; square-jawed in a varsity jacket. And then I saw Sam. He was smiling, taking a carton of milk from one of the girls orbiting around him and scratching the back of his head where his wheat-colored hair met the strength of his neck. The angles on his face were more defined now, but his dimples were still intact. And he looked stronger, almost like a grown man. Somehow he had managed to become even better looking. I could feel my checks turn red again, the very shade that had given me away years ago.

"Anyway," Julie interjected. "What exactly was Sam saying?"

JP's mouth teased upward. "Not much, really. Just asked about where you've been all this time. He remembers you, Miss. That's all. In fact, you should come out this weekend to the docks. Everyone'll be there."

I'm sure Sam King did remember me. My crush on him nearly destroyed his reputation, as if that were possible. One of his best friends, Tanya, was my sworn enemy. And now that I had the audacity to walk around campus for two whole weeks as if I were somebody new, his friends set a course down memory lane to make sure I didn't forget. The punishment due for being me was just a few tables away, and they didn't care whether I heard them or not.

• • • • •

Robby howled at the TV. "Why don't more girls dance like that around here?"

"Shut up, already!" I threw a pillow at his open mouth as he fake screamed so loud I was sure Mrs. Durham could hear all the way in Michigan.

He sprawled out on the couch with a satisfied grin, leaving Crystal and me to huddle on the loveseat, which I didn't mind. I got to inhale the scent of Johnson & Johnson's from her long, blonde hair. It was heaven. This was how we spent most nights before Denise got home from work. Robby would wait until she'd pour in the front door, reeking of spilled beer and cigarette smoke, and then he'd slip out the back before she had time to ask about homework or what we had for dinner or why the dishes weren't done.

We saw a strange sports car pull up to the house through our living room windows and knew what it meant before we even saw him.

"Where are my babies?" Denise called as she struggled to open the screen door.

Robby and I fixed our eyes on the television in defiance. Only

Crystal looked up, smiling, eager to see the mother who had just finished the late shift at the restaurant.

"Well, don't get up all at once." Denise planted her fists on her hips.

The familiar storyline continued to play out as a strange man followed her in, looking awkward and vacant and sunburnt. They always had a moustache and a fast car and never had the courage to look us in the eye for more than a second because they knew why they were there and that they probably wouldn't be back.

"This is Jim. He's a friend of mine who gave me a ride home from the grill tonight." She barreled into the loveseat and scooped Crystal into her arms, trapping my legs. "And how is my precious baby?"

Crystal kissed my mother on her cheek and pointed to her school project under the lamp. "See what I did!"

"That's wonderful!" Denise cooed. I wondered if she'd remember it tomorrow.

The middle-aged man swayed awkwardly by the front door until Robby stood up, jaw clenched. "Here." He forced the words out. "Take my seat. I'm outta here anyway."

"And just where do you think you're going, mister?" Denise called after him. But it was too late. It was Thursday night, and I knew Robby would be gone until at least Sunday morning, stopping in at odd hours for T-shirts and cereal and whatever he couldn't find at his friends' homes over the weekend. The same thing he'd done every week since we'd been back.

"You see what I mean?" she said to Jim in disgust. "It's a school night, and I can't even control him. He doesn't respect anyone, not even his own mother."

I hid in my bedroom with the radio on until I convinced myself that everyone was asleep. I opened the window, popped out the screen, and crawled to the crisp air outside. There were no lights and no sounds coming from Mrs. Durham's home. I held my breath to listen, but there wasn't a single movement—not even the rustle of a bird or a raccoon. Whatever I thought I saw the other night was irrelevant. No one was inside her house. She was still in Michigan. And I could swim again.

The wind was beginning to blow from the north. It was finally getting colder now, dipping into the forties at night, and any of the other kids raised on the island would have said it was too cold to swim. Florida cold was worse than Pennsylvania cold as far as I was concerned. Chill and palm trees just weren't meant to coincide, so every time the breeze brought goose bumps to the back of my neck, and the palm fronds bristled overhead and turned brown, something inside me rebelled. But in Mrs. Durham's heated oasis, the water was brisk and clean and the only thing I could find that could wake me up and numb me at the same time.

I slipped off my flip-flops and edged into the water quietly, as if to ensure that not even a single drop of water would notice I had invaded its space. I floated on my back, sinking my hair and my ears into the rippleless pool. The familiar smell of chlorine swept through my nose, as familiar as home and as comfortable as my bed. The moon hid from me that night; only the light from dim stars made their way through the Spanish moss and down through the mesh holes of the screened-in lanai to my eyes, where I blinked as if to signal back to the stars that I saw them too.

If there was a God, and he made these stars, tonight he was showing off.

I drifted. And floated. And when I opened my eyes again, there by the deep end of the pool was a dark figure, looming tall.

I jolted myself vertical and wrestled the water until I backed myself against the pool wall. "Oh no!" I screamed, but only a whisper escaped my lips. Water poured off of my hair on to my shoulders, and I grabbed the ridge of the pool like a shield.

"It's okay," he said quietly. He stepped around to the side of the pool and stood at the middle, leaving me enough room to run out the outer screen door if I wanted. I recognized his dark brown hair, his long jaw. It was Surfer Boy, except tonight he wore a sweat-shirt and khaki shorts, and his feet were bare, as if he had just been woken. Or, as if a burglar had just shocked him out of bed.

"Who are you?" I asked sharply.

"Who am I?" He laughed, arching his eyebrows. "Who are *you*, trespasser?"

My mouth dropped in shock. "I . . ."

"You got lost and decided to go for a swim in someone else's pool?"

My heart jumped into my throat. It was time to escape. I pushed myself out of the pool, where the cold air found me immediately, and stood there with eyes wide with shock.

"Yeah?" he said, still waiting for an answer.

"I didn't know anyone was home. I promise. I didn't mean to . . ." I stammered, searching for a way to push my heart back into my chest. "Wait a second. This is Mrs. Durham's house."

"Right."

I put my hands on my hips. "Then who are you?"

"Josh Durham."

"Josh. Durham?" I repeated. "Oh."

"Her grandson." He stepped closer. He seemed taller in the night than he did at the bus stop, and the shoulders that were once covered in the familiar softness of cotton layers now looked menacing, large, too much for me to take in.

I walked along the far side of the concrete to the screen door to avoid him. "I'm so sorry. Please don't tell Mrs. Durham—your grandma. It won't happen again."

"I don't care. But when my grandma moves back down next week, she might. How long have you been swimming in her pool, anyway?" He stepped forward as I walked backward, away from him, toward the door.

I pulled my towel around me to hide my swimsuit and caved inward against the chill. "I just ... When I lived next door a few years ago, I would go swimming sometimes. I never hurt anything. I always left it just like it was, I swear. Now I'm back, and I just thought ..."

"I know," he said.

"You *know*?"

"I know you like night swimming. This isn't the first time I've seen you, you know." A small smile etched itself across his face.

I swallowed hard, realizing this wasn't the first time I was caught in his pool. He'd given me a warning two weeks ago, and I'd been stupid enough to come back.

"Why don't you just swim at the beach during the day like a normal person?"

"Well, it's cold now. And I like to do it alone," I answered. "It's just, um ... I don't know." I swallowed hard from the lie. I knew exactly what night swimming was to me and how it made me feel. Free. And beautiful. And small. Every way I never felt in the lunchroom with Tanya Maldonado bearing her teeth in my direction, or sitting near Surfer Boy on the bus, collecting the remnants of music that dropped from his ear phones to me without him knowing.

His eyes seemed to pin me where I stood. "I won't tell," he said.

I blinked to show him my thanks. Words couldn't come.

"What's your name, anyway?"

"Missy ... I mean Melissa." I inhaled, collecting myself. "Melissa."

"You don't like Missy, huh?"

I shook my head no. "I'm sorry. It won't happen again," I said a second time.

There was nothing more for me to do than flee from this boy's lanai and hope he'd do me the honor of not watching as I slithered through my window and into my room, dripping water down the side of my cinder block home. I'd just been discovered in the last place I had hoped to remain invisible.

I looked back toward the Durham home between the darkness of my blinds. It was just feet away but seemed miles from the inside of my house, where my mother lived a lie and my brother couldn't stand it, and my sister didn't know the difference. I watched as a light from Josh's house flicked on and off, and the darkness between our rooms grew bright enough to blind us both.

Chapter 3

Could I ever fix myself enough? That's what I used to wonder in seventh grade when Ian and a pack of his clones would bark at me in the hallway. If it were just one wrong thing, I could change it. I could cover it with makeup, or go to an expensive salon, or borrow the right clothes, or carry the perfect purse, or get the right amount of tan. These things were problems waiting to be solved. But the hard reality I discovered at thirteen-years-old was that it wasn't simply one thing that they found wrong with me. It was everything.

A realization like that makes a girl look at herself differently in the mirror. Instead of looking at what to fix, I was looking for what to like. My eyes, maybe? Almond shaped, framed with naturally dark lashes. This is what the magazines said was beautiful. But in the end they were just your standard brown, nothing that could redeem my whole body. My legs, perhaps? I had swum so much that I could see the muscles on them. But muscles weren't an advantage on a girl. My eyes and my legs were the only two features anyone had ever complimented me on, and even they weren't enough to temper the fifty different ways those boys had found to let me know that I was undesirable. They were the judge and jury, and two of them sat dangerously close to me now in third period World Civilization. Only the depth of their voices had seemed to change.

"Messy." Ian whispered from his desk in the back when Mr. Miller wasn't looking. "Why so messy?"

Mike Lewis belted in a long, fake sneeze, "Ca-choo. Oh, that's messy!"

It was only a few minutes until the entire class realized what they were doing and began to giggle, uncontrollably, even if only because they knew they weren't supposed to. Before, they made fun of me because they were immature. Now, they made fun of me as if pretending to be immature. Ironic bullying — double the fun.

"I don't know what's going on here." Mr. Miller stood at the front of the class with his lips in a tight, forward scowl. "But knock it off right now."

I fought the urge to cover my face and sunk deeper into my chair until its back ridge rubbed against the base of my neck. There was nowhere to hide. The sounds of suppressed chuckles popped every few seconds from three rows behind me, and I tried to position the angle of my head far away from them, as if the information on the whiteboard at the front of class was so fascinating I couldn't dare risk looking even one degree to the side for fear of missing something.

I didn't turn my head from that board until the classroom door opened halfway through the lecture, and Sam King walked to the front of the class. Today he was wearing a preptastic ensemble featuring a blue-checkered shirt that he somehow managed to make look a little wild, as if underneath it all was some champion prize fighter. The blue was just enough to electrify his eyes, and I could feel the red blush threat working its way to my cheeks in a fury. I couldn't look behind me or to the front of the class now. The only thing left for me to do was doodle on my notepad, which was an impossible task because I was hanging on Sam's every word.

Mr. Miller: "You already took this class last year when you were a sophomore, didn't you?

Sam: "They said I could take it again, so I can improve my grade."

Mr. Miller: "I didn't realize we were doing that now."

Sam: "I couldn't get enough of your teaching the first time. I had to come back for more."

Mr. Miller snatched the paper from Sam's hand with a smirk and signed it begrudgingly. "You already missed the first couple of weeks. You better find someone to help you catch up. Take the seat behind Miss Keiser there."

I would have given anything to run out of the class and never return. The nightmare scenario was playing out just as I had feared. And with Ian and Mike perched to remind everyone in the class what they thought of me, it would only be a matter of time until Sam was pulled right back into the mix. I could handle being made fun of again, but not in front of Sam. Not when he was so close. Not in front of the one guy I'd had a consistent crush on for three years.

He slung his backpack over his shoulder and made his way down the narrow aisle. It was too tight for a football player to fit through comfortably, and I wondered how he would make his way into the small desk waiting for him behind me.

Sam approached my row and feigned ignorance. It was an obvious attempt to disrupt the class. "The seat back here, Mr. Miller? Were you saving this just for me?"

"There, Mr. King. And don't be cute."

"That's really hard for me. At least give me a goal I can achieve."

The girls in the class erupted into giggles.

Sam nodded to his crew in the back, obviously happy to have livened up the atmosphere. He looked down as he approached my desk, caught me staring, and winked.

I couldn't squeeze out a single facial expression in return. I nodded with a nervous smile and forced my eyes back to the notepad in front of me. He took his seat behind me with a thud, and I braced myself for Ian and Mike to start their comedy show over again. But they didn't.

When class was over, they piled out of the aisles and slapped each other on the backs until their hoots turned into coughs from lack of breath. That was a difference in high school. In seventh grade, they made fun of people for their survival. In eleventh, for their boredom.

I refused to think of it again until I came face-to-face with myself in the mirror the next day. Messy was staring back in the reflection, and I couldn't shake her.

I exhaled with disgust into my phone. "I have nothing to wear, and I can't leave until my mom gets home anyway."

"That's lame, and you know it," Julie replied. "Your mom will probably be home by ten o'clock, and that's exactly when we're leaving. JP will pick us up, and I'll come over beforehand to help you get ready."

I paced my bedroom like a caged woman. "Julie, I don't want to disappoint you. I just ... I don't know anyone anymore, and I don't want to be all third wheel."

She released a dramatic sigh in protest. "JP is totally fine with you coming, and people have changed. You'll see. We're not little kids anymore."

I had been too embarrassed to tell her about World Civ. "They haven't changed?" I yelled.

"Whoa, sister!"

"I'm sorry. I didn't mean to scream ... It's just that I don't see the point in standing around a boat ramp all night."

"You're being difficult. I don't know what the big deal is."

I did. If they were willing to bark in a crowded lunchroom, what would they do when I showed up at the docks, where there was nothing to stop something much worse?

"Besides, I hear that Tanya's not even going to be there," Julie offered.

"What? Why would I care if Tanya is there?"

"I'm sure you don't. But she's dating some college guy, and he's in town this weekend. That's all I'm saying."

Julie never made me beg for the information I was too proud to ask for. With Tanya out of the picture, at least one major risk factor was gone.

"You're not going to let me out of this, are you?"

"It appears not," she answered.

"Fine then."

"Okay? You're going?" Her tone brightened.

"Yeah. You're right. I need to just go and get it over with."

"Not exactly my plan, but I'll take what I can get. You're wearing something cute. It's settled."

"Thanks for inviting me. I guess." A reluctant smile crossed my lips, and I exhaled loudly again, this time in surrender.

I could just imagine Julie's unaffected grin on the other end of the phone. She was still smiling at nine thirty when she bounded through my bedroom door with two of her best shirts in hand. "This one makes you look skinny and this one makes you look curvy. What's it gonna be? Thin or curvy?" Her eyebrows arched with mischief.

Crystal jumped on my bed, pointing to the one that would make me look thin. It was white and lacy and something one of her Barbies would wear. She clapped when I tried it on with jeans. There was no refusing her. I pulled my long brown hair around to the side until it hung down past my shoulders and slathered on lip gloss until my mouth looked as plump and exotic as I could hope for.

"You were born to wear white," Julie said. "It looks so good on your olive skin."

"It looks so good on your skin," Robby mimicked in a falsetto. His head peeked through the door, and he rolled his eyes at the sight of us primping. I was surprised he'd even entered the house on a Saturday night.

"Get out!" I screamed.

"Why? What if I want to go to the docks?" He leaned on the frame with his arms folded in front of his chest in defiance.

"No boys. No brothers who smell like red tide." I raced to the door to shut it in his face. "That's you, fish master. Take a shower lately?"

"Seriously, though," Julie continued as if she hadn't missed a beat. "White is your color."

I waved her away as if she couldn't be right and pulled a cardigan on over the whole ensemble.

I had barely put Crystal to bed and Denise had barely stepped a foot in the door by the time we rushed out of the house. "And where are you going?" she asked.

"Out," I answered quickly over my shoulder. Julie's eyes grew frozen, wide with fear that our night might end before it started. She had forgotten how it worked in my house, and I began to feel embarrassed that I lived in a home where "out" would have suited just fine. Denise always left it to me to take care of myself. But that was something Julie couldn't understand; even though her parents liked to party, they still seemed to care enough to try to find out if Julie was going to be somewhere, and with someone safe, and expected her home by curfew. I added another few sentences for her sake. "Just hanging out with Julie and her boyfriend, JP."

"Well, have fun," Denise said. I had given her Julie's name and that was all she needed.

We jumped into JP's pickup. Julie took the seat in the middle and swung her legs over mine so that he could shift.

"Here, take my coat." JP pulled his varsity jacket over her lap. She looked at me and bit her bottom lip as if to say, *Can you believe he is my boyfriend?*

I studied the jacket and the varsity letters that were stitched to its panels. "I didn't know you lettered in something, JP. What sport do you play?"

"Track. It keeps me in shape for surfing." He shrugged as if the letters were nothing to him. "You didn't know I was a jock, did ya? I'm just full of surprises, girl."

The docks were nothing more than a boat access ramp and a small gravel parking lot, bordered with mangroves and smelling of the salty sweet Manatee River that danced at high tide and flowed into Tampa Bay. There was nothing more exciting there than an overweight pelican looking for dinner. But that night, with dozens of us pulling in by the minute, it was the only place to be. There were too many cars at the docks, so many that the gravel lot filled to the brim and cars spilled down the residential street where respectable people kept their homes.

We might as well have been double dog daring the cops to bust us.

Julie attached herself to JP's arm as he talked to kids I had never met and took swigs of whatever they passed him in a red plastic cup. It was foreign to see her this way: boyfriended. The last time we had hung out in middle school, we were pouring over a teen magazine and dreaming about when we would be old enough to stay out after dark. I stood awkwardly beside her as a nearby car blared hip-hop, and somewhere under a tree a group of boys had divvied out a loot of their dads' cigars and emerged in a cloud of smoke.

I felt like a creep for sticking so close to Julie, as if I were attached to her by an invisible tether—my only line to safety. Finally, I wandered to a group of girls who looked halfway friendly and listened to them recount with impressive detail where they found their outfit and how their hair was finally cooperating now that it was cooler and the humidity was gone. And Julie was right—Tanya wasn't there. No one stared too long. No one barked. And no one paid any attention to me, exactly as I wanted. I began to feel proud for standing on my own until JP and Julie barreled their way through the safety of my girl circle just minutes later.

"You look thirsty!" JP thrust a cup in my direction.

"Oh, no, I'm okay." I shrugged.

Julie pushed JP's red cup away from my lips and kissed him on the cheek. "She doesn't want your cooties."

Unable to resist her cuteness, JP turned to her and kissed her sweetly on the mouth.

"Will you two get a room already?" Sam yelled from across the parking lot. His eyes burned through them until they stopped, wiping their lips with bashful smiles. He walked over to us as if he owned the place, as if he was the host of the grand dock party, and we were his favored guests. All of the girls stood up a little straighter and tilted their heads as he approached. They offered coy smiles and wide eyes that willed him to look their way. I tried to look the opposite direction.

When I was in seventh grade, a time where girls measured boys in terms of cuteness instead of hotness, Sam was the one *everyone* dreamed about. With older brothers who had paved the way before him, Sam knew how to dress, walk, and even how to mask his voice when it was changing. He was boy band perfect, which is exactly what you want when you're barely a teenager and the decision on where to spend your affection falls between the guy who sits across from you at lunch and the guy on a poster plastered to the back of your bedroom door.

But Sam wasn't a boy anymore. He was a guy. A full-on guy, with a mind of his own that wasn't content to follow his brothers' path. I could see that now. And I could also see that not every guy had weathered the transition from cute to hot as well as he did. Ian Owens was one example. Across the parking lot, I could see Ian cutting jokes like a jester, practically begging for attention, not like the most popular guy in school he once was. Ian had hit his growth spurt early on and had been surpassed by all the other boys in our class since. I wondered if his razor-sharp comments were the only thing he had left. The fact didn't keep him from barking at me in the lunchroom, though.

But Sam, who had never seemed to expel one ounce of effort to fit in with the crowd his entire life, had never barked, and he had never said an unkind word to me. And maybe it was his silence that taught me to hope. Now, he topped over six feet, a force to be reckoned with. His hands were calloused from football practice, and his jaw was square and hard. But he hadn't outgrown the boyish appeal that seemed to glow all the brighter whenever girls were in his vicinity. And they were always in his vicinity.

"Who's this?" He tilted his head toward me as if he hadn't just sat behind me in World Civ the day before. And winked.

"You know Missy," JP answered. He buried his nose into Julie's hair as she leaned against his shoulder, but Sam was clearly dissatisfied with his answer. JP was going to need to provide some more information, or at least pretend like Sam needed him to. "She went to middle school with us." He paused for a second. "Missy Keiser. Robby's sister. Remember?"

Sam took another step forward, dangerously close. I could see the pores on his nose, the smoothness of his face, tan from a day working outside at his father's car dealership. "Oh, yeah, I remember." He smiled slyly. "Welcome back."

Thankfully, it was night, and he could not see me blush. But I knew if he stayed in front of me for much longer, I would somehow give myself away, sealing my doom. I looked to Julie for rescue, but she just raised her eyebrows as if to tell me she was completely helpless to save me from the situation.

"Where you been all this time?" Sam asked.

"Pennsylvania."

His eyes narrowed. "Why?"

"That's where my mom's boyfriend was from."

"And now y'all have moved back? Did you get sick of the cold?"

"Yeah. I mean, it was cool to get to see snow. But they broke up. So now I'm back home." The word *home* reverberated through me like a gong.

"And now you look . . ." He smiled.

I braced myself for a stinging remark, but it never came.

He bit his lower lip and shook his head with a grin. "I can't believe it's you, here." He pushed his red cup into my hands. "Have some."

Our conversation was over. He left me with a cup of brown, frothy liquid and turned to JP.

I can't tell you if I heard the siren or saw the lights first, but all I remember is that suddenly every student ran like ants scattering from a hill. They bolted back to their cars and into the neighbors' yards in a panic, taking their beer and cigars and letterman jackets with them.

The flash of the cop car lights lit up the graffiti on the side of the storm wall. Our high school letters were tagged on the concrete in spray paint, as if the cops needed any help figuring out where to find us.

I ran toward JP's truck, but he and Julie were already far ahead of me and climbing inside. Julie sank down low into the front seat as if she were making herself invisible to the officers. She climbed over JP to get into the driver's seat and pushed him to the passenger side, likely because he had alcohol on his breath. Music blasted from car stereos as everyone turned on their ignitions, jolting the neighborhood dogs from their sleep at the sound of the chaos.

The few seconds I hesitated to run had already cost me. Just as I started for the getaway truck, a police car swung in front of me. The officer shined his high beams right on the red cup in my hand. I froze.

"Get in!" I heard a voice shout from behind. A silver Buick had pulled up behind me in a rush.

"Huh?" The beams of the police car blinded me. I couldn't see JP's truck anymore.

"It's me. Get in the car—*now*!"

I dumped the red cup, splashing its contents, and jumped into the car. When I looked to the driver, Josh Durham was reaching across me to shut the passenger door. He threw the car into drive and we rushed out of the lot. The lights of the police cars shrunk in the side mirrors until we made it to Manatee Avenue and turned back toward the island.

"Do you ... Do you think they got your plate number?" I struggled for my breath.

"It doesn't matter. I wasn't doing anything wrong." Josh's voice was quiet, even.

I could smell the beer that had landed on my sleeve and knew I couldn't say the same thing. "Thanks for helping me."

Silence.

"I came with JP and Julie. I was trying to get into his truck, but the cops' lights were so bright I couldn't find it after a while."

The right corner of his mouth turned up in a small smile. "I know. I watched you freeze."

"Well, they're probably worried about me. They're likely still waiting for me."

"Or not." His mouth turned up at the side, but I couldn't tell if it was a smile. "JP saw you run to my car. They know you're with me."

"You know JP?"

"Of course," he said. "You're the new kid, not me. But you can use my phone to text them." He must have assumed I didn't have a cell. Robby and I both actually had our own phones, even if we didn't have much else. They were the only good things either of us got to claim from her Pennsylvania boyfriend, except for Crystal. I pulled mine out and made a show of texting Julie.

I could feel exactly nothing from Josh as he drove us through the narrow streets without a word. We rode in silence over the swampy marsh of Perico Island and across the drawbridge until we were back on Anna Maria. He drove past the mom-and-pop motels, and the liquor store, and the city hall with the shuffle board court in front. We passed all the places of our town, places we knew independently of each other but now saw them together for the first time, for the first time at night—all in utter silence.

These things were clean and familiar during the day. But at night, in a car with a strange boy, the walls looked like they were trembling, just waiting to fall down and reveal a strange new truth inside that high school kids never get to see.

We pulled into his grandmother's driveway, and I could see the blue light from the television in my house flickering from my living room window next door. I wondered if Josh was going to raise the garage door and drive into his grandmother's home with me in the passenger seat. Would he close the door behind us? Should I get out now?

He turned the ignition off as the car sat in the open driveway and leaned his head against the back of the driver's seat. He looked at me for the first time. "It's nice to see you again. Dry this time."

I shut my eyes in embarrassment. "Thank you ... again. I'm not typically breaking rules, you know?"

"Pool hopping isn't breaking a rule?"

"I guess you have a point." Silence again. I balled my hands into a fist to keep from biting my nails. At least if I could bite my nails I could hide half my face, so he couldn't see how awkward I looked. How I had nothing to say to him. How I was fighting the urge to ask him so many questions. "So why are you here, anyway? I mean, I used to live next to Mrs. Durham years ago, and I never saw you."

Josh ran his hand through his shaggy dark hair and looked at me square in the eyes.

"I lived in town."

"Yeah?" I said, waiting for more.

"And now I don't," he said. The bottom part of his jaw shifted to a side, making the angles of his face look unearthly or masculine; I couldn't decide.

"Okay. I wasn't trying to be nosy." I reached for the door to leave.

"I'm not trying to be difficult. I just don't usually talk a lot."

I smiled at the confession. "You shy or something?"

"Something like that," he said. "It just takes me a while to talk around people, I guess. The reason I'm out here on the island now is that my dad remarried, and I thought ... We all thought it would be better for everyone if I moved out here. That was in eighth grade. I've been here ever since."

"You didn't like her?"

"I just wasn't part of her plan."

He looked around the car as if he was hoping something could distract us. "But it's okay," he finally said. "My dad and I are good. I see him a lot. I like the beach anyway, so I don't miss his house too much. And my grandma is actually pretty cool. She just wanted an extra couple weeks up north with my cousins, so I'm here alone. I get to use her car when she's not around."

Most people I knew dreamed of having a house all to themselves, but I could hear in Josh's voice that being left alone had lost its novelty a long time ago.

"I'm not totally off the leash," he added. "My dad comes by to check on me. Like random inspections or something."

"And your mom?"

He swallowed hard as if he was collecting the right words in his mouth. "She's up north. After the divorce, I guess there wasn't enough in Bradenton to keep her down here. I see her a few times a year. She's not in the picture that much."

I nodded. "Yeah, I know what that's like."

"You do?" he asked.

"I never met my dad. Not that I remember, anyway."

He looked to my house and then back to me. "I'm sorry."

I shrugged in response.

"And Robby's your brother?"

"Yeah," I answered. "Same dad. Robby thinks he remembers him, but I don't remember anything, and we're only a year apart. My mom says he took a job in another town one day, and he never came back. No one knows if that's really true, but that's the story she tells us. She claims the only thing he left us was our ability to get a good tan. He was some part Cherokee, so Robby and I can stay out in the sun longer than her. She just burns."

Josh smirked as he pulled up his sleeve to compare his forearm to mine, even with only a streetlight to see by. I scrunched my cardigan up past my elbow. The sides of our arms touched, and I was suddenly aware of the warmth of his skin.

"You do have a pretty good tan," he admitted. "Better than mine, and you just got here." He moved back to his side of the car. "Robby's a good skim boarder. He sticks to himself, but I've seen him down by the piers since you all moved in. Finally, we have some waves. And the little blonde girl?" The sides of his mouth curled up at the mention of her.

"She got to you too, huh? That's Crystal, our half-sister."

"She's pretty adorable. I saw her in the hardware store the other week asking everybody if they had seen Mrs. Durham. She didn't quite get it when I said that I could help."

The breath left my chest with a gush. I was outed. "Well, she probably thought you were some kidnapper or something." I looked away in hope that he wouldn't see right through me.

"At first I wondered why a little girl was looking for my grandma, and then I remembered that I had a visitor the night before. She was probably scouting to see if the pool was off limits for a certain someone." He smirked. "You saw my grandma's Buick in the parking lot and were trying to see if she was back yet, huh?"

"Guilty." The bottom right of my lip twitched downward.

"I'm on to you, Missy," he said dryly. "I mean Melissa."

"That's okay. Everybody remembers me as Missy, so I can't hide from it. You can use that name too."

"So, why do you sneak into little old ladies' houses and use their pools, Melissa?"

"I'm really sorry. I really didn't mean to be weird. It wasn't like I was trying to break in. I just ... Something about a pool, especially at night."

I shrugged my shoulders, supposing that he didn't really need an explanation, but he didn't flinch. His dark eyes met mine and his mouth was at rest. He was listening.

"I just like to swim is all."

His mouth twitched. "That's not all. People go pool hopping all the time around here, but they usually stick to condos. You were staking out my house. You even had your little sister involved. That takes effort."

"You really want to know?" I stalled. "I like to be alone. Not at some hotel where other people are around. It makes me feel free. Like somehow I'm suspended above everything that—"

"That tries to pull you down?" I could tell from his tone that he wasn't making fun of me.

I exhaled begrudgingly. All of my secrets were out now, swimming around us so to speak, and there was no more room in the car for anything else. And if I didn't do something, I was going to have to return to a house where Denise was likely not alone if the vehicle now in our driveway was any indication, and I couldn't escape. I looked down to his right hand tensing on the console. I imagined Josh wanted to drive us both away and never come back. I imagined him fighting the urge to turn on the ignition and drive us over the drawbridge, and past the cops still harassing our friends at the docks, and beyond the sandy dirt of the orange groves out east.

The veins popped from the top of his hand and wrapped around his forearm, browned and sculpted from a fall semester spent skim boarding.

He swallowed hard and his Adam's apple jumped at attention in his neck. "We better get to bed."

My imagination took a nose dive. He wasn't thinking of any of that. "Big day tomorrow?"

"Something along those lines."

The question had come out of my mouth before I could stop it. I hated being sarcastic, but it was the only defense I had managed to build in the face of rejection. Here was a boy who had me in his car, parked in front of an empty house and a vacant pool, and he was sending me home. I knew there was no reason for me to think I was being rejected. I hadn't offered him anything. But something was clear between us. He had a wall, a boundary, and he was not interested in crossing it.

"Thanks for the ride," I said too casually. "See you around."

I settled into my bed as the scenes from the night played over in my head like a movie. There was the boy next door who seemed to be keeping me at arm's length, and there was the boy I thought would never step in my direction, who might possibly have just been pulling me closer. Josh Durham and Sam King.

I awoke the next morning to the sound of Mrs. Durham's garage door opening at the unseemly Sunday morning hour of nine o'clock. I peeked through my blinds to see Josh backing up his grandmother's Buick and taking the car toward the island's north end, where nothing of interest was located. Just outside my bedroom window, waiting on the ledge that bordered the glass, were my two flip-flops. Josh had returned the shoes I had left beside his grandmother's pool.

Chapter 4

Even in January, the Florida sun was bright enough to force my head to bow in surrender. The glare ricocheted off of the white shell driveway and into my eyes with an unmerciful violence.

At first, all I saw was the figure of a thin man walking toward me with a slight limp, like he had an ache in his back from working too hard. It wasn't until I saw Crystal running toward him with arms wide open that I knew I had been wrong. The man had never worked a hard day in his life.

"Daddy! Daddy!" she yelled.

"How's my baby?" He lifted Crystal into the air and laughed as she smothered his stubbled cheek with kisses.

"Yay! You're here! You surprised me!"

"Your mom didn't tell you I was coming? I called her last week."

I guessed why Denise hadn't mentioned Doug's impending arrival. She wasn't counting on it.

"Hey, Missy." Doug turned to me with a wink. "How you likin' it back here in F-L-A?"

It's great. It was wonderful having two days to pack up our things in Pennsylvania after you and my mother broke up for the third time. And we had to relocate. Again.

"Fine. Florida's fine." I shifted my weight to inform him the conversation was finished. I wasn't interested in small talk or hearing about whatever quasi-legitimate business deal he had going or how he met some celebrity at a tiki bar in Orlando.

"Yeah," he nodded. "I missed it too. I couldn't stand living back in P-A after all." His eyes grew wide as if he was going to explode if he didn't give the reason for his visit. "I'm movin' back, you know. Did your ma tell you about that?"

Say you're not going to move in with us. Please say you're not going to live in our house.

"Down to Fort Lauderdale. I got a job laying sheet rock."

I let my exhale of relief escape too loudly. "Fort Lauderdale? I hope you got your manelry ready."

"How's that?"

I tried to keep the smirk from overtaking my face. "Man jewelry. All the Yankees down there wear lots of gold and drive cars they can't afford. It's the uniform." I could feel my behavior slipping, and I needed to leave before I got worse. After all, Crystal was standing a few feet away.

I turned my back on Doug and headed inside to the living room, where Robby was pounding on the top of the video game console to get it to start. It was the first time I had seen him since Thursday night.

"Guess who's here," I announced.

Robby grunted. "I saw. He better not come inside."

Doug remained a safe distance from our front door and pretended interest in Crystal's bicycle, marveling at her ability to ride up and down the block with her training wheels. He made no effort to teach her how to ride the bike without the trainers. I'm sure he knew he wouldn't be around long enough for the lesson to stick.

"Mom!" I yelled. "Get up! Doug's here. He's out front with Crystal."

"I'm coming." Denise emerged from her bedroom in cutoff jeans and an orange tank top that showed off her figure. She was still young, although I didn't appreciate that fact, and pretty, even in the morning without makeup and her hair slung back into a ponytail. I looked nothing like her.

"What is he here for, anyway?" I crossed my arms in front of my chest and followed her into the kitchen. The mere presence of Doug was enough to turn our house upside down.

"He owes on child support. He better be here to pay up."

"Well, he says he's got a job now, and he's moving back to Florida to take it." I turned toward the couch to sit next to Robby and ran straight into the chest of a tall, somewhat fit man. I looked up toward his pointy chin in shock.

"Oh, sorry about that. I didn't mean to be in your way." He smelled of my mother's shampoo and a fresh dose of mouthwash that wasn't working well enough. Beads of water from a recent shower dropped from his wet hair and onto his Hawaiian shirt. He was yet another perfect stranger who had just stumbled out of Denise's bedroom.

"No, baby," Denise cooed to him. "You're not in the way. The only one in the way here is my ex, and he knows it. That's why he's not coming inside." She walked past me in a hurry and kissed her latest fling on the cheek. "Robby, Missy, say hello to my friend, Ray."

I met my brother's eyes as he sat with his controller in hand. Each of our mouths hung open slightly, as if we were working to inhale what little oxygen was left in the room. Our mother had orchestrated another train wreck, and there we were in the middle of it. Irrelevant cargo.

"Hi, kids. Nice to meet you," Ray said without extending his hand for a shake. His eyes crept from my mom's retreating form toward the front yard where Doug was pacing impatiently. He must have realized he had no choice but to take a seat on the couch near us, where Robby was now fixated on destroying a three-eyed creature and pretending that Ray didn't exist.

It was my cue to exit. Somehow the situation inside my house was less comfortable than standing outside with Crystal and her deadbeat father. I poured myself a glass of water and left Robby to entertain our new guest.

"Is your mom coming out or what?" Doug motioned toward the door that I'd let slam behind me.

"I think so."

After several uncomfortable minutes, Denise floated out of the house in a gray cloud from her lit cigarette. "About time you showed up."

"I got delayed," he said.

She blew smoke out with a hard push as if she was trying to kill the gnat that hovered near her forehead. "I was expecting you yesterday."

"Well, I'm here now, and I'd like to take the little one down to Fort Lauderdale with me for a day or two."

Crystal's blue eyes grew wide. Her father had come for her.

"She's got school on Monday," Denise answered. "Responsibilities. Heard of 'em?"

"A day or two won't hurt her. I'll have her back by dinner Tuesday night."

I placed my hand on Crystal's silky blonde hair, stroking it as she pleaded with our mother for permission to go. It didn't matter to Crystal that the day we left Pennsylvania, Doug spent three hours at a tavern a block away, leaving us to load up my mother's minivan on our own. It didn't bother my sister that he didn't come home in time to hug her good-bye, or that he had so far mentioned nothing of the two boxes of her toys that he'd promised to ship down weeks ago but had never shown.

"How on earth can I trust you to take care of her?" Denise arched her eyebrows as if she was looking forward to his response. "You haven't even kept up child support. And I don't see you handing me a check now."

"Well, it's not gonna be just me down there."

"Oh, no!" Her voice had grown loud enough to stop everyone within a two-house distance. "You have some hussy down there, do you? You're not letting some other woman around my little girl!"

Crystal grabbed on to my legs and buried her face against my hips.

"She's not a hussy." Doug clenched the side of his jaw in a weak show of restraint. "But that's not who I meant, anyways. My sister is down there staying with us too."

"Well, aren't you father of the year!"

"I don't want to hear it from you, Denise. Would you rather I take off for a gig and never come back? No one would blame me if I did!"

The reference to my father punched me in the gut.

Denise swallowed hard as her eyes darted to me and back to Doug. "How dare ..." The front door slammed shut again. Ray was making his way to the carport with his arrow of a chin pointing into his chest as if he was hoping he could escape without being seen. Someone should have explained to him that a grown man could never be invisible in an orange and red tropical shirt.

"Who's that?" Doug asked, pointing wildly.

"No one," Denise answered.

Ray stopped in his tracks at her words and then shook his head. He continued on to the carport to retrieve his motorcycle.

"I mean ... no one to you!" she corrected. She rushed to Ray's side and stroked him on the back of his neck. "I'm sorry, baby. He'll be out of here soon. Don't go."

Ray shook off her hand and fired the engine of his bike until it released a loud rumble that echoed in the grass-carpeted alley between my bedroom and Josh's house. He drove down our driveway, onto the street, and past our neighbors' homes until he disappeared from view. Denise watched him ride away with a look of genuine shock on her face. She returned to my side with her lips in a tight, unbroken line.

The vein on the side of Doug's jaw popped out in protest. "A friend of yours?"

I reached around Crystal's shoulders and started to lead her back to the house. She'd seen and heard enough.

"I want to go with daddy," she cried. "I want to see Aunt Kathy."

Doug pointed to Crystal as if the protests of a seven-year-old were evidence enough that he was indeed a good father. "See that? Just until Tuesday."

Denise threw her cigarette into the grass and turned away as it released a thin fume above the blades. Her daughter was crying to leave. Her man had left. And her ex was on his way to South Florida with another woman. "Fine. Take her."

I stood there as Crystal raced into the house to pack her bags and Denise followed behind in silence. From deep inside I could hear Robby's game explode over the television speakers. One of his soldiers had crashed and burned. I realized just then that my mother had known all along what would happen — that Doug would arrive this morning. That he'd sweep in with big plans. That she needed to show that she had a man inside the house in order to face Doug outside of it. That it had all backfired when her latest fling got fed up sitting next to a resentful teenager and waiting for a woman who was only interested in playing games.

The white beam of sunlight blinded me through my eyelids again. When I opened them, Josh was standing beside his grandmother's Buick next door. He was silent: his face intent, expressionless. I averted my eyes to escape his stare and turned my attention to the cigarette still smoldering in the lawn. I poured my glass of water over top in disgust. Before Josh could begin to speak, I returned inside my house. There was no explanation for what he had seen, and so there was no reason for me to try to invent one.

"I'm getting out of here for a while," Robby said to me. "Wanna come?" I followed my brother into his makeshift bedroom, where he sifted through mounds of dirty clothes and unopened schoolbooks. When he finally found his wallet in a pair of crumpled jeans, he tugged on my arm to follow him out. It was the first time he had invited me anywhere in a very long time.

"Where to?" I asked.

Our eyes met, as if somehow we both realized in that moment that we were each other's only witnesses. No matter how well we learned to tell our story, no matter how much time we could put between us and this day, we were the only ones who would ever know what it was really like to be standing there, hearing Denise on the phone pleading with Ray to come back, watching Crystal pack her suitcase for a father who would never be good enough for her, and wondering what kind of man gave us our last name, and where he was now.

I stood on the back tire pegs of Robby's bike and hung on to his shoulders as he raced us down Holmes Boulevard to the marina. He had owned a car in Pennsylvania, but it couldn't make the drive to Florida without breaking down. He'd told me he was at least another six months from having the money for another.

"You remember Bruce P?" he yelled over his shoulder to me, nearly out of breath from pedaling.

"Yeah. Mom's regular at the restaurant?"

"Yeah, well, he's giving me a few hours of work as the bait boy."

"That's good. He actually pay?"

Bruce Paczkowski controlled one of the oldest marinas on the island, and his family claimed to have been here since the Spanish landed. Yet no one could pronounce his last name or even spell it, so the islanders called him simply "Bruce P." He had given up trying to convince them of anything different. It was rumored his own business cards read simply *Bruce P* and that city hall kept duplicate records on his operations, filed under both names.

As we pulled up to the docks he owned, the smell of fish and salt water sunk deep down my throat until I felt like I needed a shower.

"He pays me for running the bait. But it's not just about that," Robby said.

I jumped off the bike as he let it fall to the gum-stained sidewalk. He barreled down the seawall toward the wooden dock that lined the canal. Sailboats and motorboats floated proudly in their slips as pelicans perched on top of wooden moorings. At the end of the dock the water was brown with murk and seaweed congealed at the surface, baking in the sun. Robby hopped over a boat lift and led me to a patch of grass behind the office, well out of sight from the tourists.

"Watch the prickers."

I dodged the sandspurs that tried to wedge their way into my shoes and followed my brother to a skiff that was propped up on cinder blocks behind the bait shack. It was a small boat compared to the cruisers around us, and it was missing a motor. But I could see that someone had been working to scrape the barnacles off of the bottom.

"What's this all about?" I kept my distance, half expecting a stray cat to leap from the pile of rotting wood.

Robby squinted in the sunlight and let out the first smile I had seen from him all day. "It's gonna be my charter."

"Huh?"

"Well, Bruce just wants me working the bait for right now. But he's letting me work on this boat on my own time. He has an old engine for it inside the house. And he says I can use it when I want if I can get everything up to par. Maybe I can even take it out for fishing trips this summer. You know, with the tourists. He'll take a cut, and I get the rest."

I circled the boat. Knee-high weeds brushed its belly, and the grass below had turned brown from lack of sun. It had been there awhile. "Don't you need a license to take out tours?"

"Whatever." Robby shook his head dismissively and his eyes narrowed on mine. "Not everything around here needs to be on the books. This boat's not big enough to do deep sea in the Gulf, but I can get around the bay just fine. Probably fit four men and their gear on it, plus me. The mackerel and red snapper come into the bay just the same as they do on the Gulf side. And no one's gonna say boo to me doing a charter now since the oil spill. They're just glad to see us out there." He stopped himself as if waiting for my response.

He had a lemon, for sure. It was an old fisherman's money pit, and it had been paraded in front of my brother like a golden goose. I chewed on my thumbnail as I tried to make sense of it. "So, he's paying you to work on it?"

"No," Robby answered with a sigh. "I'm making a little money as the bait boy. But this is an investment. I give him my time on it, and he gives it to me to use with the tourists once it's ready. And he's teaching me about things at the same time. Like, last week I went out fishing with him and he showed me about netting finger mullet for bait."

Robby circled the boat to scrape off more barnacles from the hull. I had never seen him more focused on anything, other than skim boarding. I could see why the Brits and the Yankees would pay my brother to take them out. They'd love to meet a real island kid, someone who knew where to spot dolphin and how to catch tarpon. Robby's blue eyes would sparkle from the glints off of the salt water and tourists would be paying hand over fist at the sight of his boyish grin—a perfect mix of vulnerability and mischief.

"Well, I think it's great." I nodded with approval and ran my hands across the bow until a piece of paint peeled off underneath my finger. "You'll make a lot of money in tips too. Have a car in no time, and then I can stop riding the bus to school."

Robby beamed. "This is it, Missy. This is gonna change everything. Once I start makin' some money, it'll be different. This whole island will feel different because we won't be stuck. And I can't wait to take that bay on. All I need is a boat, and I'll rule it."

"Take it on?"

"Yeah," Robby shrugged. "You know, man versus sea."

We stayed on the docks all day, so by the time we returned home Denise was already at work and the raccoons were beginning their nightly scavenge through the backyards. It was too quiet to sleep, especially with Crystal gone. I thought of the events of the morning. How Josh stared back at me as my family imploded on the front lawn in full circus mode. How he looked like he was taking a mental picture of every last detail, tagging each of us in his mind with the roles we played. The Great Keiser Family Dysfunction. Now Josh knew more about me than most of my friends. And in the face of this, he stood there in silence.

I had just put my hair in a perfect messy ponytail when I peered through my bedroom window blinds toward his house. Somewhere behind the cinder blocks, the wordless surfer was doing his homework or listening to some painfully cool college band just because he liked the beat. He was certainly not thinking of me.

And then I saw something gleam in the moonlight on my outside window ledge. I raised the blinds and held a lamp up to the glass to make it out: a small silver key. It hadn't been there earlier in the day. The only explanation was that Josh had left it for me just like he had left my flip-flops. My window ledge had become my personal mailbox.

I threw on a sweatshirt and tiptoed outside on the grass to reach the little key. It was less impressive in the cup of my hand than it had looked through the window, even too small to fit in the front door of a house. And yet it was left on the ledge with no explanation. No note. No instructions. And then I realized ... it must be the key to his grandmother's lanai. The breath punched out of my lungs as I imagined why. It was a pity gift. He had left me a key so that I could escape to his pool.

I wasn't too proud to take it.

I didn't even bother to put on street clothes. The screen door to his lanai was firmly shut, and there wasn't a sound or a hint of light from his house. There wasn't one clue that he was awake. Perhaps that was his gift to me, the understanding that I could use the pool if I could be just as quiet as him.

I rushed back to my bedroom, threw on my swimsuit under my nightclothes, and returned to the lanai to try the key. The hole in the screen door I had once used to pull the latch from the inside was now patched. Without a key, there was no way for me to break in without damaging his grandmother's door. Although I never would have taken my trespassing that far, Josh had given me a way around it. Tonight, at least, I could rationalize that I wasn't an intruder. He had invited me to the only place I could find some peace. I was a guest, even if neither of us could ever fess up to the fact.

I waited for him to appear through the sliding glass door of his living room and step beside the pool. I waited for a light to go on, a dog to bark, some acknowledgment that I was there, that he was my accomplice. But he didn't show. Finally, I held my breath, slipped the key into the lock, and turned.

It didn't budge. I tried again, and it still didn't give. The key didn't fit.

"What is up with this?" I whispered to myself.

"Because it's not made for that lock," a voice said from the darkness. It was Josh.

I stepped backward as he walked out of the shadows and toward the door to meet me on the other side of the screen. He wore a plain white T-shirt and board shorts like he had spent his afternoon in the Gulf and let the clothes dry right to his bones. If he was cold in the night air, he didn't show it.

"Did you think I gave you a key to my grandmother's house?"

I was mortified. "No."

He grinned.

"I mean, I don't know. I guess."

He opened the screen door and walked past me toward the backyard before stopping. I followed like a lap dog.

"Don't get me wrong," he said, turning toward me. "I would love to give you the key to our pool, but I generally try not to give my grandma a heart attack. She gets back tomorrow night."

"So?" I shrugged, holding up the key in confusion.

"So," he answered. He pounded a flashlight against his palm and gestured for me to follow. We walked to the back of his property line and through the unfenced yards of the next two houses until we reached a new lot, bordered by a makeshift wall of thick shrubs and trees. He shined the flashlight on the ground until I could see the roots and mounds we'd have to dodge as we walked about fifteen feet into the brush. Finally, we reached an old cottage hiding behind a frame of yellow hibiscus whose blooms had already shriveled for the night. Spanish moss dangled from above and dripped on to its tin roof. I had never noticed this house before. It was out of place, from an era when the locals still had to take ferries to get to the island. It looked abandoned.

"This cottage has been in the family a long time. It was the old winter house when my grandma was a kid. Now, it's a seasonal." Josh pointed to the lock on the chest-high, wooden gate that formed a large rectangle behind the cottage.

"So you rent it out for the winter?" I looked over my shoulder. No one would think to look for us here. Houses on the island were built on empty sand lots, not wedged between oaks and palms as if the building itself were an inconsequential addition to a perfectly good swamp. I had passed this lot every day but had never imagined a house was hiding at the end of the winding, dirt driveway that poured from the main drive. "Is anyone here?"

"No. This year she hasn't been able to get a renter. So it'll probably be empty until the summer."

The wind kicked up and a chill brushed the backs of our necks. Josh shivered. A temperature in the low fifties was intolerably cold for Gulf residents, and it was clear my Pennsylvania blood had definitely adjusted back to island level. Especially since I was only wearing my pajamas.

"Go ahead," he said.

I put the key into the lock and pushed the gate open slowly. I stood at the entryway, unwilling to take another step.

"So now you're suddenly shy about going on to someone else's property?" He led me through the gate, and we stepped on to the mulch that formed the cottage's backyard. With a few more steps, we arrived at a small pool that almost glimmered. Josh squatted next to the water and felt the temperature with approval. "Gran keeps this pool heated with solar panels as well, which is about the only modern thing on this whole property. It still has a rotary dial phone inside."

The tiles around the pool's perimeter were a 1950s pastel blue, as if we had gone back in time and invaded some abandoned Hollywood mansion. Its side wall had sustained a long, thin crack, and the shape of it curved in and out like a lagoon. It wouldn't be an easy pool to swim, but if I cut across the length diagonally, I could get in several good strokes with each lap.

"What do you think?" Josh tilted his head to wait for my response.

"You're giving me a key to this gate? Are you telling me I can swim here?" My whisper cracked in excitement before I could finish the question. It was a dream.

"Whenever you want. Should be all yours until July," he said. "Just don't let anyone see you. The only person who's supposed to be on this property other than me is the pool man."

"This is amazing!" I searched his face. His eyes seem to be smiling but his jaw was locked, slightly crooked as he studied my reaction. "But why are you doing this for me?"

"I just thought you'd like it."

I stopped short. It was hard for me to look him in the eye. If I stared at him too long, he might notice what the other boys did. That I wasn't pretty, not up close, not even at night. I distracted myself from the thought. "I do."

I dropped my nightclothes to the concrete to reveal my swimsuit beneath. I got in the water to hide my body as quickly as I could and felt the familiar cool of the water paint itself up my spine. The pool may not have held any feelings for me, but I was in love. Its stillness offered more peace in a few minutes than I could get in days at home. I swam underwater to the far end and caught my breath.

"This is so awesome!" I laughed at the thrill of it.

Josh bit his bottom lip with a smile and placed the key and flashlight next to the pool's rim.

A dangerous, unspoken hope rose up from my chest. It was the first nice thing a guy had ever done for me. "Are you coming in? It's not cold once you get in."

He dropped his eyes to the concrete ridge. "I better not."

He wasn't going to swim? I stopped treading water and made my way to the center so I could get closer to him. "It really is warm enough."

"I gotta get back. Look, just don't get caught. And don't let anyone else swim in here. This has got to be a secret." He met my eyes and forced a smile. "Promise?"

"Of course," I said.

The gate closed tightly behind him, and I could hear the crunch of the leaves and grass fade into nothing as he walked away from the cottage. I was incredulous. It made no sense for him to risk getting caught and not even have fun himself, even if the goal wasn't to have fun with me. I pulled myself out of the pool and let the water of my new refuge stream down and collect at my feet. Josh had given me a gift. And he had left me alone to use it all by myself.

I went there most nights over the next two weeks.

• • • • •

Mr. Miller had been to every continent on Earth, and that even included Antarctica, which meant he began every new chapter in our textbook with a slideshow of one of his trips. Mr. Miller on an elephant in India. Wrapped in scarves on a mountain in the Andes. Wearing a fanny pack in Paris. His eyes would sparkle as he told about getting out of Bradenton and touching the shrines built by men thousands of years ago. And all of this would be fascinating to me too, if only I could stop trying to look out of the corner of my eye.

Finally, Sam leaned forward from the desk behind me and whispered in my ear. "Fanny pack."

A burst of goose bumps erupted on the back of my neck as I felt his breath slip through the back of my hair.

"You know you want one. That fanny pack is so hot."

"And the best trip of all," Mr. Miller announced, "was the trip I took to Inner Mongolia, where I went to the Mausoleum of Genghis Khan, which is just south of Dongsheng . . ."

"Dongsheng?" Sam mimicked. "Is that contagious?"

I suffocated my laugh so Mr. Miller wouldn't look our way. But I had giggled just loud enough that the boys who were heckling me just a week ago were elbowing each other at the sight of Sam whispering in my ear. A certain smile pulled at my cheeks that I couldn't shake until class ended.

Before the class emptied, Sam leaned forward to speak to me again. "Hey, did you get those notes?" His dimples poked inward like two signposts marking their way to danger.

I couldn't respond.

"Hello?" he asked again.

Wake up. "Um, yeah. Yeah. Dongsheng. Got it."

"Mind if I borrow them? Just for a night. I couldn't focus today."

I began nodding my head in agreement before he had even finished his sentence. I popped open my three-ring binder and handed them over. "Here. And here are the notes from last week too, for the quiz on Friday."

"You're the best," he said with a wink. And in a moment he was out the door, wrapping his arm around a redheaded cheerleader. I could hear her giggle bounce off the walls.

By the end of the week, Sam had not returned my notes. I forced myself to ask for them back at the end of class on Thursday.

"You thought I forgot, didn't you?" Sam said, shaking his head in jest. "Missy, Missy. I know you need to study for the test. Don't worry, little one." He handed the notes back to me and pulled them back to tease me as I reached for them.

"Give 'em," I said with a smile.

He placed them in my palm and pulled them back again.

"You're kind of annoying, aren't you?" A full smile broke across my face, and I gave him what I hoped was a charming glance.

"I think you love it." He cocked a brow, looked around, then whispered in my ear, "So, you should come over tomorrow night."

"Huh?" I asked.

Before he could answer, Ian and Mike were making fart noises at Wayne Dubowsky as he tried to squeeze down the row from his seat. The squeeze wasn't easy for Wayne.

"Hey, Dubowsky. When you go to a restaurant, do you just look at the menu and say, 'Okay'?" Mike yelled.

Wayne's freckled cheeks grew red.

"Hey!" Sam yelled. He looked at Mike and Ian like they were small children he needed to scold.

The rest of the room hushed. One word from Sam had redeemed Wayne and silenced the peanut gallery that rumbled from the back of the room. Even Mr. Miller tried to conceal a small smirk. Wayne smiled with satisfaction as the boys shrugged off Sam's reproach. And I saw for the first time just what it meant to be Sam King. He had power to redirect attention wherever he wanted. He had the power to tell his own friends to shut up and protect a chubby bandy geek just because he felt like it. If he liked you, you were anointed. You became immune, like he injected you with his personal Sam King vaccination against all the high school crud you could otherwise never escape.

"So ..." He turned back to me. "Like I was saying, you should come to my party tomorrow night. It won't be that big, but it'll be a good time."

"You want me to go to your party?" I hated that I sounded so shocked. The world had started spinning in reverse direction. What would his friends say? What would Ian say when I walked through the door? Would he bark?

He smiled, as if he enjoyed seeing me nervous. "Yeah, if you want."

I pursed my lips to buy time so I wouldn't look too eager. "Okay. I think I can make it."

Sam responded with a quiet laugh and nodded his head. "Good."

He rose from his desk without a second look.

I had never been so eager to get to the lunchroom. Julie and JP would be able to tell me if the invite was legit.

Before I could introduce the idea, however, JP crashed into his seat and began chugging his chocolate milk. He took a break between gulps and said, "So, you guys are in for Sam's party, right?"

"Huh?" My chest deflated in disappointment. Apparently, Sam had invited everybody else too.

"I'll pick you guys up at nine."

Julie met my eyes and elbowed JP. He got up and left the table as if by some unspoken command. "You look like you're doing algebra right now, not talking about a party. What's wrong?" she asked.

"Nothing, I'm just trying to figure it out ... Sam invited me. Like *personally* invited me."

Her eyebrows raised and a wide grin erupted across her face. "Really? Well, that's good, right?"

"Yeah, but I didn't know everybody was invited."

"You are crushing on him!"

"Am not."

"Are too!"

I gave her the big eyes that are universal in girldom everywhere. She needed to lower her voice before someone like Tanya Maldonado overheard.

I started to bite my nails. "He talks to me sometimes. He never used to do that before. It's like all of a sudden, ever since the docks, I exist."

"Missy," she said, pulling my hand from my mouth. "You don't get it, do you?"

I looked around as if she was going to point to something important. "Get what?"

"You're totally hot now. And you've been away, so now it's like you're the new girl." Her eyes went wide. "You're like the *hot* new girl. You're totally Bella."

I shook my head and looked around at the tables of people buzzing with lunchtime gossip. Half of them wouldn't let me sit with them if it were three years ago. "Julie," I whispered. "Are you forgetting I'm Messy Keiser?"

"Are you forgetting Sam King crossed the docks to say hi to you? Are you not seeing that *Messy* doesn't exist anymore?" Julie tucked her light brown bob behind her ears and waited with her mouth open in anticipation.

"Doesn't exist? Just two weeks ago I was sitting in World Civ and they were calling me Messy again. And you were right here when they started barking in the booths. Sam was there too, remember. Maybe this whole thing is a joke. Maybe it's just a prank to get me out there."

"You've seen too many high school movies. They were talking about history. And, frankly, they were probably just trying to get your attention. You can rule this school now. I mean, you've blossomed. Or something. Whatever it is, no one but the most immature idiots remember that girl anymore."

I sunk back in my chair as the weight of what Julie was saying reached through me and tickled my stomach. I couldn't accept it, but I could see that she was intent on getting me to believe it.

"You're my best friend, Julie. You're required to give me pep talks like that. But really, the best thing you could do for me is to keep me from crossing the path of all those same guys again. If they started teasing me now, I don't know if I could handle it. I just want to get through graduation and get on with my life."

Julie shook her head in frustration. "Really? Is that the reason you were so excited when you sat down? Just trust me. There's a reason Sam invited you to his place."

JP came back to the table with more of his buddies in tow. A party planning committee began to swarm around me as each of them talked about how they were getting to Sam's house and what they were going to do. I had never been at the center of so many of the populars before, and it wasn't long before Tanya Maldonado came up to our table on her way out of the lunchroom.

"Hey, Tanya." Julie said, as if she were our table's hostess and required to greet our new guest.

Tanya nodded as if it was an effort.

"This party's gonna be killer." JP wrapped his arm around Julie's shoulders. "You going, Tanya?"

“Maybe.” She sighed. Her focus turned to me, as I pretended interest in the rectangular slice of pizza on my plate.

Julie spoke up. “Tanya, do you remember Missy?”

“Hey,” I said, swallowing hard.

“Yeah, of course I remember you.” She blinked heavy and smiled brightly—overly brightly. “Great to see you!”

It was the Southern Special: the fake nice. The only question left was whether she still had it out for me.

“Are you going to Sam’s house too?” Her features stretched with innocence. And then, as if stumbling upon a great realization, she said with a wink, “Oh, right. *Sam’s* house. Of course! Yeah, I guess I’ll see you there, won’t I? I’ll bet you wouldn’t miss that, now would you?”

Question answered.

Chapter 5

The loud thump of dance music escaped Sam King's house and rattled down the length of the block, shaking windows and leaving the rest of the song behind somewhere inside. JP parked his truck in front of a stranger's house, where a man peered at us through his window as if we were criminals. There had to be thirty cars parked along the curb of the street, and I knew it would only be a matter of time before the cops came to bust us up and send us back to our respective corners of the school district.

JP shook his head as if he was looking at an old lady. "Why do you look so tense, Missy? We're fixin' to go to a party. Get it?"

I nodded quickly as if to agree. Sure, I was fully on board with the fact that I was about to go hang out alongside Tanya Maldonado and Ian Owens and Mike Lewis, all of whom had sat at a cafeteria booth barking in my direction just days before. At least Leigh and Brett would be there too, and they would have to be nice to me on account of Julie and JP. My numbers were at least up to four. Walking into that house was going to be like navigating a rat maze. But there was one person I was hoping to find at the end of it.

Julie leaned over to my ear and whispered, "He invited you. Personally."

I tried to fight a tough girl smile at the thought of it.

"What is the issue with you two?" JP pressed. "We should be out of this truck and walking down the street."

Julie turned to her boyfriend and revealed the secret in the sort of way that only a best friend could. "Look, these are your friends. But not all of them are our friends. Especially Tanya Maldonado, and I know she's gonna be in there."

JP grimaced at the thought. "Seriously? That's why you girls are all spun up? Tanya's still popular only because no one bothered to ask why she shouldn't be. No one really cares what she says anymore. We're juniors now. I mean, everything else is history."

History. I wanted so badly to believe it, but the sounds of a terrier running loose in the cafeteria reminded me that some people had not forgotten.

Julie kissed JP on the cheek to reward him for his encouragement. We walked through the garage door of Sam's house that led to a converted rec room. I wondered if he would acknowledge knowing me now that we weren't in the safety of World Civ. I pulled at my top, wishing that my clothes were cuter and that I was thinner in them.

No sooner did we pull ourselves through the door when every girl in the house flittered into the center of the room to dance to some bubble gum song that was so girlie sweet it made me feel like I were covered in glitter. The boys rallied around them with approving stares and fake danced to the chick music as everyone let out high-pitched screams.

JP came to rescue Julie and me with plastic cups full of beer in his hand. He held them out as if we had asked for them. When I looked around, I realized we were the only girls without a drink in our hands. Julie took a cup first, then I grabbed the other. We sniffed the liquid and grimaced at the pungent smell. It was horrible, masculine.

"It'll taste better if we hold our noses," she yelled above the music.

This time, I didn't fight the idea of drinking what was inside one of JP's red cups. I was, after all, entitled to party like everybody else. And the cup in my hand was like a license to be there, hanging out with people who inexplicably accepted me into their circle.

I swallowed the beer and felt a rancid taste fill my mouth. The stench snaked up my throat and through my nose, and I wanted to be sure that no one stood too close to my breath. Then I realized why I hated the scent so much and why I associated it with older men and dirty bathroom floors and fish and chips. It smelled like my mother after a Friday night shift.

I held the cup for the rest of the night but didn't take another sip. I pretended to drink it when I needed to. And I pretended not to be hiding when Ian stood too close to me near the ping-pong table, or I pretended to be smiling when anyone looked my direction. Finally, it was way past our curfew, and I was tired of pretending.

I turned to Julie and tried not to look too eager. "Shouldn't we get going?"

She shushed me with her finger.

"I'm serious. It's gonna take another twenty minutes to get back to the island." I whispered into her ear. "It's not my mother I'm worried about. It's yours." I raised my eyebrows until she pursed her lips and set the red cup down.

Just then I felt a hand on my waist. When I turned to see who was touching me, I came face-to-face with the bluest eyes I had ever seen. His arm had fully extended around my back, and he hooked me close to him until my lips were close to his cheeks.

"Sam!" I exclaimed with too much exuberance.

"You having fun?" His hand lingered around my side, at the small space where my skin was exposed above my jeans. It would have looked as if we were dancing together, except by now the dance music had faded and the speakers were playing a slow, whiny song where the guttural voice of the lead singer seemed to cry out everything I was too proud to say. Sam squinted his eyes as I collected myself.

"Having fun?" I said. Suddenly, I was. "Uh, yeah. Great party!" I tried to keep my eyes from growing too wide at the thrill of his arm around me. In public.

"Good. I'm glad you came. It's nice to see you out." He winked, stepped away, and went upstairs to where he must have been hanging out all night. Apparently the football team was trying to create a makeshift wrestling match that needed his attention.

Julie stepped toward me and met my eyes in reciprocal shock. Sam's hand had been on my waist for eight seconds. I tried to fight the nervous smile that wanted to take over my face and excused myself for the bathroom. I waited in a dark hallway for it to free up, which was probably a good thing since I might not have been able to have a normal conversation with another human being. And then Tanya, as if smelling blood in the water, glided down the corridor and planted herself directly across from me.

"Hey, there," she said.

My heart jumped into my throat. I had almost made it the whole night without having to see her. "Hi."

"It's great to see you here," she said. Her eyes were wide and her teeth gleamed underneath the soft illumination of the hallway light.

"Yeah, it's good to see you too, Tanya."

"So, I didn't know you liked to party."

I nodded and forced my mouth to curve up slightly.

"Do you like to go to parties, Missy?"

It was an odd question, particularly the way she said it. Slow and pointed and falsely perky. But I knew exactly where she was headed. She did the same thing in middle school. It was her patented interrogation tactic. She didn't hit you with hard questions, but with basic ones, ones that made you feel like a fool for answering.

"Yeah," I answered. "I guess."

"And at Sam's house. Do you like being here? At Sam's house?"

I nodded yes.

"Mmm. I'll bet. I mean, it's fun here with the rec room, especially since his parents are usually gone." A small smile crossed her lips, and I watched how they curled into a perfect cupid shape under her perfectly thin nose. Why did she seem to dislike everything about me when I did nothing but admire her?

"I like your shirt," I offered, hoping to change the subject. "The cut looks great on you."

She nodded as if barely tolerating my compliment.

I hated myself instantly for praising her. I hated when girls used compliments as defense weaponry, and I hated that Tanya didn't seem to be aware of the fact that Sam had placed his arm around me for eight whole seconds.

Finally, the bathroom was free. I went inside and left Tanya to wait in the hallway. Before I was finished, I checked myself in the mirror and remembered how she'd told the other girls I might have bugs. How she led the entire class to begin calling me Messy. Before I realized what I was doing, I began scouring the bathroom to make sure it was in good order before I left it for her. Toilet lid down. Sink wiped. Towels straightened. I found a long, brown hair on the tile floor and wiped it up with a tissue, just in case it was mine, just in case Tanya would see it and think it was mine. When I finally opened the bathroom door, she was leaning against the hallway wall with her arms folded and head tilted to the side. I should have let her use the restroom before me.

It was one in the morning by the time I made it home. Denise hadn't bothered waiting up, which was fine because there was no way I could explain where I had been and why my breath wreaked of hops—that is, if she even asked. I tried to settle in for sleep, but my mind was jumping with questions that sleep wasn't going to answer. And I didn't want to rest yet. There was no guarantee that the feel of Sam's strong forearms around my waist would be as real when I woke up. I put on my swimsuit underneath a pile of sweats, grabbed the key, flashlight, and a towel, and headed for the cottage pool.

It looked amazing, twinkling under the full moon. But there was so much more to distract me from it tonight. For the first time since I arrived back on the island, I didn't crave the escape of the water like I always had. The thrill was subdued, sleeping underneath the frenzy of being invited to a party by Sam King, who winked when he told me he was glad I came. And maybe, also, there was just a bit of anger bubbling inside of me at the fact that Tanya Maldonado had unhinged me in a matter of two questions. I had actually lowered myself to cleaning a bathroom so that she couldn't have an excuse to call me messy. I was sixteen, but in that moment I might as well have been back in seventh grade.

Anger, and not just fear, began to boil within me. I should have asked her a sweetly snarky question right back. I should have asked her why she liked coming to Sam's house since she supposedly had a hot college boyfriend. I should have asked her if Sam personally invited her too.

As I pulled off my sweats and dropped my towel by the gate, I was overcome with the sense that night swimming was beginning to feel ordinary. There was so much else going on.

"You haven't been here in a while, huh?" a voice asked.

I jumped in my skin until I saw Josh standing in the dark under the cottage's back porch awning. He was shirtless, stuffing his towel and shoes on a lawn chair. "Oh, wow. Josh, I didn't see you!"

"I know." He released a crooked smile as if he had just gotten away with a practical joke. "But you didn't answer my question."

Josh walked toward the pool and stepped down the shallow end stairs. His muscles were lean but defined, at least for a few seconds until he submerged and they disappeared from view. A jittery feeling welled up within my stomach at the sight of him. When he raised his head above the water again, I had still not moved.

"I guess I haven't been swimming in a couple of days," I admitted. "I've been busy."

"Well, you're here now." He nodded toward me as if to let me know it was okay I was there. He hadn't called dibs on night swimming. I could join. "It's not cold once you're in."

I sat on the edge of the deep end and slowly slipped into the pool. I leaned my hair back into the water and smoothed it down. As I waded in farther, I pretended that it wasn't chilly outside, and the longer I stayed in, the more that was true.

"So," he asked. "How was Sam's party?"

"Good. How did you know about that?"

"I was invited too. Did you have fun?" He swam to the middle, and we treaded water next to each other.

"It was alright. I had a decent time," I answered.

"Did a lot of people show up?"

I narrowed my eyes at his questions, but his face was at an easy rest. He wasn't interrogating me like Tanya. He seemed to genuinely want to know if I enjoyed myself, as if he was taking a survey of what captured my attention. "It was pretty packed." I looked at Josh closer. "I didn't realize you were friends with Sam."

He looked to the fence as if something had distracted him, but I could tell he was disappointed that the conversation had flipped to him. "I've been friends with Sam since preschool. Our dads are pretty tight."

"Really? So, why weren't you there?"

"Busy."

A short laugh escaped my lungs. Most of the kids in our class would have fought each other for an invite to that party. Beer. No parents. Three unchaperoned stories with girls dancing like they were auditioning for a rap video. I pushed myself closer to him for the inquisition as we stirred our arms in circles to stay afloat. The water moved between us in miniature whirlpools, rippling with our movement. "What else could you have been busy with on a Friday night?"

He tilted his head as if to tell me it didn't matter.

"I see. So, you missed out on Sam's party to hang out here at the cottage?"

Josh splashed water toward me. "Exactly. I'm antisocial."

"Well, I can tell you have your own way of doing things." I raised my eyebrows, but I wasn't just teasing. Something about Josh hinted he was powerful enough to rule that school, and yet he didn't.

He swam to the shallow end and propped his elbows on the concrete behind him in silence.

"Are you really not going to answer the question?" I pressed.

He blinked a nonresponse.

"I can tell you don't want to tell me. Which of course means I have to know. Were you on a date?"

If the moon had been brighter, I might have been able to tell if he was blushing. But the only reaction he gave was the slight lift of his top lip, as if he couldn't decide between smirking and talking. "No."

Relief swept over me unexpectedly. *Where did that come from?* "So, are you going to make me guess every possible option?"

"Nope. And you wouldn't guess this, anyway ... I was at church." The side of his jaw clenched, and he looked at me earnestly, as if he was trying to read my mind by the cut of my eyes.

"Church?" I repeated in disbelief.

Josh nodded.

"Instead of Sam's party?"

He shrugged.

Right. He was there on a Friday night when one of his supposed best friends was hosting the biggest event to happen to our high school so far that semester (and had wrapped his arm around my waist). "So, what? Does your grandma make you go or something?"

Josh shook his head no, just enough for me to see it was the only answer he was going to give. He looked to the water as if I was reacting exactly the way he expected, and pushed away from the wall to swim past me.

When he reached the deep end, he smiled and waited for my next move. But I didn't have one. I was left only with the sense that I didn't understand who he was or why he allowed me to pool-hop at his grandmother's cottage or how he could have come across as so mysterious when in fact he was just going to church on Friday nights. I suddenly felt like I was a trespasser again.

"No grandmas," he said. "It's a youth group. It sounds lame, but it's actually fun. We hang out."

"Okay . . ." It sounded like a cult. Or daycare. "I just didn't know that you were into that."

Josh propped himself against the ladder. Church boys were supposed to be soft and wear khakis every day. He was rough and, if I were being honest, appealing. The ridges and sinews that cut across his shoulders and arms showed hours of lifting a skim board, not choir books. "I didn't always go to youth group. But now I do. And so sometimes I'm at Sam's or wherever, and sometimes I'm at group. I hang out with both. It's just that the more I read the Bible and learn about God, the more I want to know."

My ribs constricted in embarrassment. He wasn't talking about the God of OMG. Or the God you thanked when you got out of summer school. He was talking for real. I almost felt sorry for him. Was this something he turned to because he never saw his mom and his dad moved on without him? Whatever the reason, I wanted out of the conversation. "Well, that's cool if you're into that kind of thing. It just isn't for me."

Josh didn't move, and a small smile etched across his lips. Was he feeling sorry for me?

I suddenly felt judged. "All that stuff in the Bible was written two thousand years ago and people have corrupted it. There's no way to know what's what." I made my way to the stairs. The conversation was getting weird, and it needed to be over.

"Well, if there's no God, then you're right," Josh said. "But if there is a God, isn't it possible that he wants us to know him? Don't fathers want their children to know who they are?"

The sentence hung in the air between us like a lightning bolt. Neither of us could grab on to either side of it.

"Not mine," I answered.

I wrapped my towel around my shoulders and headed back to my house. My stomach turned at the thought of how he sounded. Like some crazy on the TV. He was nothing like he looked. But I still took the key with me.

• • • • •

Something terrible must have happened because Denise was up too early to be cooking breakfast. But it wasn't the cooking that disturbed me. It was the sound of the cabinets slamming and dishes clanking, like there was a bar brawl over the French toast. Except she was the only person in the kitchen.

"What's wrong with Mom?" I whispered to Robby as I stepped into the living room.

His gaze slid to mine. "Hawaiian Shirt Ray came back. Mom was happy for about five minutes, until something came up about this other woman he's been hanging around with. And then he left. It all went down last night."

A pot crashed violently against the kitchen sink, and we heard Denise yell, "Good for nothing! You're all alike! *You're all alike!* Who's that talking? Is that you, Missy? Don't you ever trust one of those good-for-nothing louses. They'll leave you for the next woman in an instant."

Robby couldn't laugh this one off. He wouldn't help her anymore, either. I could see it in his eyes; he was finished with Denise's failed relationships. We both knew she was making a scene so that one of us would make the mistake of trying to comfort her. It always ended with one of us saying something wrong, and Denise shrugging off our hug or stabbing us with eyes that killed. We were no different than all the men that left her, she'd say. We did nothing but take from her, she'd accuse. And within minutes she'd have a new target for her rage. But this time neither of us took the bait.

"I'm outta here." Robby scratched his messy brown hair and tucked his skim board under his arm. "See ya."

I glared at him. "Where have you been lately, anyway?"

"Nowhere." He shrugged.

I looked out the window, where a somewhat familiar vehicle was idling. "You've been hanging out with Ricky Brewer, haven't you? The stoner?"

"Whatever." He let the screen door slam behind him and jumped into Ricky's car.

I pulled Crystal into my room to save her from Denise's implosion. By the time I finished painting her toenails, Denise would be calm enough to take care of her again. Crystal picked out the light pink polish with glitter, and I laid an old towel beneath her feet as I began her pedicure.

"Mommy's mad." She peered up at me with wide eyes.

"Yep," I said. "But she's not mad at you. She's mad at that guy, Ray."

She was always mad at some guy. And the reason he left was always his fault somehow. Too into himself. Too afraid of being a stepdad. Too lazy. Within moments after every failed relationship, Denise would rattle off the reasons it didn't work out as if she had known the man was worthless from the very first date. The reasons were never that she jumped into bed with him too soon. That she picked a drunk in the first place. That she expected him to act like a husband after the first week. That she never quite stopped flirting with her backup candidates just in case he didn't work out or he turned out not to make as much money as she thought, after all.

But none of these excuses fit my father, it seemed. He was the one mystery in our family. Robby talked about him like a war hero, a man who cooked pancakes and took us fishing. He hugged us every night, and he gave us special nicknames. Even though Robby was only one year older than me, the few memories he had grasped in those early years were enough to give him a sense that someone out there had made us one-half normal. We had one regular, loving parent. The theory never sat well with me considering that one regular parent ran out on us, at least the way Denise told it.

The truth was Robby had conjured up these memories from a mix of one or two real-life incidents and a whole boxed set of saccharine sitcoms. The father Robby had cooked up was nothing but a figment of his imagination, unequal parts family idealism and a four-year-old's hazy recollections. Our dad was little more than a ghost. But, to me, the idea that he might be a good man and had still left us alone made it sting all the more. Robby's memory haunted us just enough to know that we should feel shortchanged he had left us. It was as if we knew just enough to know we missed him.

My mother's reaction to all of this perplexed me. I could feel her words dig into my mind. *They're all the same. All the same. And they all leave us.* Yet she never stopped striving to find the one who wouldn't.

Crystal stroked the stuffed dolphin her father had bought her in Fort Lauderdale, and I worked hard to push back the feeling of jealousy rising in my throat. At least her deadbeat dad loved her.

The phone rang. Julie's voice started before I even finished the word hello. "Guess what!"

"What?" I wished I could match her exuberance, but I couldn't summon it this morning.

"JP just called. Sam's having another party tonight."

"That's cool. Are you all going?"

"Are *we* going?" She sounded like she might explode if she didn't finish her story.

I started to laugh. "Why are you being so weird? What's going on?"

"Sam texted JP to tell him about the party and that he should be sure to bring ... you."

I jolted up at the news. "What?"

"He's asking about you, Missy!"

"Nuh-uh." I tried to swallow but my mouth was suddenly dry. "Well, I'm sure he was just being nice. I'm sure he told JP to bring lots of people."

"And then he texted .... 'she's cute.' "

"As in me? Cute?"

"Yep," Julie confirmed. "JP and Sam are friends and all, but it's not like they hang out every day. Sam texted JP out of the blue. And this party tonight is supposed to be a smaller one. Missy, he called you cute. *He called you cute.*"

I walked over to the mirror and tried to determine if Sam was joking. Could he have actually meant it?

"Missy ... Hello? Are you still on the line?"

"Um." I tried to keep my tone even, faking disinterest. "I guess I can make it."

Barely a second later we both laughed out loud, and I jumped on to my bed in a nervous fit. "Oh my gosh, Julie! I— "

"I know. You've totally crushed him for, like, four years, and now he's crushing on you back, and you guys are gonna be like Bradenton royalty. Wills and Kate!"

We exploded in giggles at the thought. Crystal jumped on to my bed to join me as if somehow she knew. Maybe even seven-year-old girls could tell when a girl had just gotten good news about a boy.

A couple hours later, once the blood had returned to my feet and quiet settled back over the house, a forty-something man walked to our front door holding a ten-dollar bill for my brother.

Denise's dark mood brightened instantly. She invited him in, and he marveled aloud how he could never get over the fact that Robby had such a young mother.

"Missy, you know Bruce, right? He's one of our favorites at the restaurant, and your brother is doing some work for him at the marina."

I nodded my head and kept my distance as the two made their way to our kitchen table.

Denise fluttered around the kitchen to make a cup of coffee. "He came to drop off some tips Robby forgot, for cleaning fish for the tourists. Wasn't that nice?"

I tried to make sense of the scene unfolding in our house. Who was this strange, happy woman talking to me? Wasn't she still slamming dishes and cursing men just moments ago? Now she was laughing too loud at Bruce's stories of catching mullet with his bare hands and showing gray-haired tourists from Quebec how renegade nudists would park their boats at Bird Island. Denise lit up as if she had just discovered a pot of gold.

She took a seat next to Bruce and propped her chin on top of her hand like a schoolgirl. "I've lived here almost all of my life, and do you know I've never been out deep-sea fishing?"

"Well, any woman on the island should know how to deep-sea fish," he assured her. "We'll have to remedy that."

The man didn't have a rope to save himself. Bruce was a hearty, barrel-chested man with black hair that thinned into a perfect, bald circle at the top of his head. His hands were thick, and the broadness of his shoulders made him look taller than he actually was. He carried himself like a king, and I could tell the reason he was sitting at my kitchen table was to get Denise to believe he was.

My mother served a piece of the crumb cake she'd taken home from the restaurant and laughed easily at his remarks as if Crystal and I hadn't just been confined to our rooms in order to avoid her man-hating tirade. Before I could think to text Robby that his boss had come by to drop off his tips, Denise's hand was already resting on Bruce's shoulder. The tides changed quickly with Denise, and it was all I could do to stay afloat.

I fled to the front yard to escape. I sat on the grass and pulled my hair out of a ponytail to let it collect warmth from the sun, and tried to calm my breathing. Moments later, Josh road his bike toward the house from the direction of the beach with a skim board under his arm and a body suit folded down around his waist. It was too late for me to go back inside. He threw his bike and board in front of his garage and walked toward me until his knees were level with my eyes.

From the looks of him — drenched in salt water with sand glued to his calves — he had already gotten in at least an hour's worth of skimming. He shook his wet hair over me. I exhaled to show my annoyance.

"What's up?" he asked.

"Nothing." I shrugged as if to make my lie more believable.

"The waves are up today. For the Gulf, anyway."

I pretended to study the grass and plucked the blades with my fingers. I knew if he stayed there another minute he would bring up last night's awkward conversation. Or he'd see Bruce P come out of my front door — the third man to leave my house in the matter of as many weeks. Neither was okay by me. I only had to make it a few more hours before Julie would come get me for Sam's party, and then I could forget everything that had happened that wasted Saturday.

"Your brother got down there just as I was leaving," Josh continued.

"Good."

"I'll be glad when we can ditch these bodysuits in a month or two. The Gulf was cold today." He towered over me until I looked up. His face was still glowing from his swim. "You okay?"

"Perfect," I said.

Josh looked around, into the darkness of my house through the screen door and toward the street where Bruce P's SUV was parked alongside a ditch. His eyes narrowed for a brief second. And, just when I thought he was going to surrender and go inside, he lay down next to me on the grass and propped his hands behind his head.

The water from his suit ran on to the blades below us, and I could smell the sea on his skin. I pretended not to care that he was so close, my folded knee just inches away from his stomach, so close I could feel the warmth of the electricity firing between us. He didn't seem uncomfortable with the silence I was trying to create. And I couldn't decide if I liked it, any of it.

I heard the screen door shut behind us and the sound of my mother's laugh carry across the yard. When we turned to look, Bruce was strutting like a giant down my driveway. My mother called out to him, "Can't wait until tonight!"

Josh turned to me. "Is that . . . ?"

"Yeah."

"And doesn't Robby work for him?"

"Yeah." I raised my hand to bite a nail but fought the urge.

"So, are they—?"

"As of five minutes ago, probably."

Josh closed his lips in silence.

Crystal skipped out of the house and followed Bruce to his SUV. He reached through the window and handed her a small white object before driving down the street. When she walked up to Josh and me, she was hiding it behind her back.

"What do you have, little sis?"

She grinned mischievously and shook her head as if she wouldn't give up her secret.

"Come on," I prodded. "What did Mr. Bruce give you from his car? Josh wants to know too. Don't you want to know, Josh?"

Josh sat up and nodded dutifully. "Definitely. But it looks like it was probably just a white piece of paper. So I wonder if it's even cool."

The challenge was enough to get her to reveal her treasure. Crystal dramatically revealed the new gift. It was a white sand dollar, and a large one at that. Josh and I oohed and ahhed as she stroked the flat, circular shell with her finger.

"It's not alive anymore," she explained. "It's dead. It was bleached by the sun."

A smile pulled at Josh's lip as he rubbed his finger on the smooth surface.

"Do you know the story of the sand dollar?" she asked. "I learned it from my friend at school."

We shook our heads no and sat up straight for the lesson.

Crystal pointed to the grooves on the sand dollar. "Well, this design on the top part here is the outline of an Easter lily. And see the star shape in the center? That is for the Star of David. And on back, when I flip it over, that's one of those red Christmas flowers."

"Wow! How do you even know what all that stuff is?" I asked.

Crystal twisted from side to side in a show of pride.

Josh nodded in approval. "That's very cool, Crystal. And you know what else I heard? I heard the best part is that, if you want, you can break it open. And inside there are five doves of peace."

"Birds?" Crystal asked. She turned the shell in wonder as if looking for signs that little doves would pour out.

"Well, they're more like small little shells inside, but they look like doves."

Crystal shook the shell and we heard something rattle inside. "They won't come out."

Josh pursed his lips. "Well, that's the hard part. If you want to see them, you have to break the hard shell."

Crystal clutched the sand dollar to her chest. "I don't want to."

"You don't have to. Not unless you want," Josh reassured her. "But when it turns warmer, I'll show you how to find more sand dollars on your own."

"Then I'll open it. I don't want to break it until I have more."

I elbowed Josh. "Where'd you learn about the doves?"

"Youth group." He smirked.

"Naturally."

He leaned slightly back on his hands. "You're rethinking your decision not to go with me sometime, aren't you?"

"Almost," I said.

By the time Crystal and I headed inside, Josh had helped me forget about my mother's sideshow act. I actually felt at ease. And I could imagine why he went to a place where it was okay to tell stories about sand dollars, or whatever it was they did there. No one was slamming dishes. No one was calling the ugly girl names. No strange men were stumbling by. It was safe. Even if it wasn't real.

I wondered what it would take to feel that at peace all the time. Or even better—loved.

When I shut my eyes, Sam's face appeared brilliantly in my mind.

Chapter 6

I'm going out tonight. You'll need to watch your sister!" Denise yelled from the bathroom. The perfume and hairspray and cigarette smoke swirled down the hall and into my bedroom.

"Mom, please! I have plans!"

Something checked me in the gut, but I stuffed it down. If Robby had a problem with our mother dating his boss, he'd have to take it up with her. It was time for me to get ready for Sam's. If he thought I was cute, I was going to try to look the part.

"You what?" She poked her head through my door to inspect me. "With who?"

"Julie and JP and ... Sam King." I said his name just to see how it felt coming out as an answer. *I have plans with Sam King.*

Something glimmered in Denise's eyes. "Sam King? Who is *that*?" She stretched out the word *that* as if it had cooties.

"No one," I lied, pushing down a smile. "And don't use that ridiculous voice with me."

"Well?" Her eyes were wide with mischief.

"It's just a party."

"And?"

"Sam is just a boy."

"Just a boy, huh? Well, you look real pretty for just a boy." She moved to my side and stroked my hair. "You've been keeping an eye on Crystal all day. Maybe I'll stay in tonight. I'll invite Bruce over here."

"Okay," I replied, waiting for the catch. But there wasn't one.

"I hope this Sam is good enough for you." She tucked her thumb under my chin and brought my eyes to meet hers. "Don't be stupid like I've been. You deserve a good guy."

I didn't know how to respond, and was glad when she finally left and I could finish doing my hair and makeup. JP and Julie picked me up just after dark, and we headed in town to Sam's house, where a line of pickup trucks and hatchbacks were pulled neatly into his driveway so as not to attract attention. The lights toward the front of the house were off, so none of the neighbors could see how many kids were packed inside at the back. This was going to be a quieter night.

I followed JP and Julie up the stairs from the rec room entry and into the main part of the house, where a country song slipped out of speakers in the ceiling. There would be no hiding behind the ping-pong table tonight. Leigh and Brett waved to us from the kitchen table, where they were playing cards with a few jocks. Through French doors that opened off the side of the living room to the porch, I could see Ian and Mike sitting beside Tanya and a few of the others in her crew.

Anger at the sight of her warmed me from the inside. *Yes, Tanya, I like going to Sam's house. And I am here. Just like you. And I was invited. Just like you.* A part of me wanted to go sit beside her and show them all I wasn't Messy anymore, but I knew I didn't have the courage. I just wished I didn't have to see them at all. If they stayed out on the porch, I could join the game around the kitchen table and be just fine. I was here for a reason that they had nothing to do with, and he was walking through the door.

"What's up, people?" Sam hollered as the guys swatted him with high fives. He glided through the room passing out smiles like carnival tokens. "How's it goin', JP? Glad you could make it."

JP nodded. "Someone had to teach these guys how to play cards."

Sam filled a pitcher with beer and leaned over the kitchen table to set it in front of us. "And I see you brought some beautiful ladies." He winked at Julie and Leigh.

JP wrapped his arm around Julie's shoulder protectively. "Watch it, Romeo. This one's mine."

Sam smiled until his dimples appeared. "No problem. But I'm first in line after this kid, got it, Julie?"

Julie laughed. "I'll remember that. And you should too, JP." She kissed him on the cheek to show she was teasing.

"Okay, I'm headed out to the porch. But you all have fun." Sam placed red cups on the table and turned to me for the first time. "And relax. Enjoy yourselves."

JP grabbed two cups and passed them to Julie and me. "I'm driving, so you two have at it."

Relax. Have fun. That's what I wanted most. To be able to hold eye contact with Sam for more than two seconds without flushing pink from embarrassment. For the next two hours of the party, all I really remember is the fact the red cup in my hands never seemed to get empty. Every time I took a sip, someone topped off my glass. I barely noticed when most of the other people went home.

Sam took an empty seat next to me and peered over my shoulder to see my hand of cards. "Is this the first time you've ever really drank?" His grin made me feel like a little girl.

"Maybe," I admitted.

"I can tell, because there's no way you should have a hand like that at this point in the game." He pulled a card from my grip and laid it on the table.

"Rookie mistake," I said. I pushed the card to the center of the pile as everyone around the table grimaced at my move. Apparently it was a good one.

He raised a satisfied eyebrow. "So, you having a good time?"

"Definitely." I nodded with an exhale. I couldn't get the chant out of my head. *Missy, he called you cute. He called you cute.*

Through the doorway to the porch, I could still see Tanya and Ian and Mike surrounded by the select few who sat with Sam each day at the cafeteria booths. This was Sam's inner circle, and I was quite possibly the newest member in it. Ian palmed a basketball, and I tried to avoid looking him in the eyes. But I could see he was watching me as Sam leaned over my shoulder to help me with the game. I didn't want to look Ian's way. I didn't want to remind him that he once thought I was so ugly he screamed at the sight of my face, or remind Mike that he had once pushed a pile of books into my chest. I had a story about all of them, like they were Hollywood stars in a movie I was desperate to forget. And now the mystery of how they spent their Saturday nights was solved, and I wasn't peeping through a window to observe from the outside. I was in the room.

JP jumped up from the table. "Let's get some music going, huh? I'm sick of sitting around." He pulled Julie from her chair and wrapped her arms around his neck for a dance.

Sam obliged and rose to change the music. He lowered the lights as the deep lull of a slow, achy song filled the room. And then, standing in the center of the floor where the kitchen melted into the living room, he extended his hand toward me. "Care to, ma'am?" he asked in his best cowboy voice.

I didn't realize what beer could do to me until I tried to stand up. I held on to the counter to collect myself. The alcohol had turned my walk into a sway that landed me, conveniently, right into Sam's arms, where he was waiting to lead me to the makeshift dance floor. It didn't take courage to hang on to him when I was already half asleep. I buried my nose into his navy blue polo shirt and smelled the remnants of cologne that had lingered at his collar. I could barely catch my breath at the feel of his chest underneath my chin.

"Easy there, sweetie," Sam said as he caught me. He wrapped his arm around my back and propped me against him, pulling me close as if he had no doubt that was exactly where I wanted to be. We swayed left to right as the Nashville singer crooned about his never-ending love. And it was easy, after losing count of how many times the red plastic cup had been filled, to believe that Sam felt the same way about me as that love-struck singer felt about his girl. Sam mouthed the words as if reciting a poem, and I felt the top of his arms station themselves underneath mine like branches of a live oak. When I was ready to stumble, he was able to hold me steady.

Somewhere behind me, the stairs creaked with the weight of a visitor. I didn't look to see who had come into the room until Sam stopped swinging to the music.

"Well, look who's here!" Sam bawled. "I thought you were too good to come over!"

Josh walked into the living room with a face that gave nothing away. He was freshly shaven and matched Sam in a yellow polo shirt. He looked like any one of the guys sitting around the room, preppier even, which didn't fit his normal uniform of a black T-shirt and cargo shorts with a chain dangling from the pocket. Tonight he looked no different from any of the other jocks in the house, although I knew they hadn't spent their morning on a skim board or maybe their afternoon reading the Bible at some church. Nothing about Josh fit in with this crew.

He barely nodded in my direction as he took a seat at the table next to two other girls who lit up when he said their names.

Sam broke free from our dance. "Man, I'm surprised you made it! You never come to these things. Want a beer?"

"Naw." Josh looked down in his typical shyness. "I'm cool."

"Of course."

I had been abandoned, dropped like a rag doll. Everyone hovered around the kitchen table to pour more drinks and to ask Josh why he hadn't been around lately. I was too proud to fawn over him. I wandered around the bookshelves in the living room, intent on ignoring the fact that I had just been ditched mid-dance thanks to my next-door neighbor. Not to mention Mr. Holier Than Thou would smell the alcohol on my breath and never talk to me again.

The wood shelves were crammed with framed photos of Sam's family, each person more beautiful than the next. It was a funny thing about rich people — they always looked good in sterling silver picture frames. The pictures showed parents and siblings and cousins leaning in to each other with big side hugs and perfect, white smiles that matched the bleached sails of the boats behind them. There were pictures of Sam through the years, and many of them showed a young, dark-eyed boy by his side. The boy's eyes were unmistakable. Josh wasn't just one of Sam's friends; from the looks of these pictures, he was a part of Sam's extended family.

Their friendship was the reason Josh could walk into a party full of preps and jocks and be just as welcome there as he would be on the island, at a party with my brother and his dazed, disheveled friends who always smelled of salt water. As I watched them at the kitchen table poking each other with their elbows, I realized I was the outsider to this relationship. Josh hadn't crashed my party. I had crashed his.

Sam waved me over to the table and wrapped his arm around my shoulder. "So, Josh. Have you met Missy yet? She's new. Kind of."

Josh sucked in his lower lip. "Nice to meet you."

I turned to Sam with a smile. "We're neighbors, actually. I live next door."

Sam shifted in surprise. "Girl next door, huh? Josh, you've been holding out. You didn't tell me you had a new neighbor."

Josh shrugged and pushed some cards around the table.

"So, Missy, what's it like to live next door to Josh? Is he staring in your window at night? Gotta watch out for him. Like a wolf in sheep's clothing, that one."

Before long, the rumble of the conversation lulled and a couple had passed out on each other's shoulders on the couch. I excused myself and headed for the bathroom upstairs.

When I was finished and made my way to the dark hallway, I felt the weight of the alcohol sweep down my body and knock the strength out of my knees. I held on to the wall to stabilize myself until Sam came to my side to keep me from falling over. He wrapped his arm around my waist and told me to grab on to him.

This is what being drunk was. Though it made me feel strange and unsteady, it was the only thing that gave me the confidence to be in Sam's arms, to sit in a house full of people who used to laugh at me. It was the only thing that made me feel important.

Sam King called me cute, and now he was holding me, pulling me closer as if I were his girlfriend. All I could do was focus on the collar of his shirt, because it was the only thing in the hallway that wasn't spinning.

"Come this way." His hands were rough, hardened from football. The giant mitts of his palms swallowed my fingers and pulled me to a study that featured two long leather couches placed on opposite walls.

I sunk into the cushions of the closest couch and closed my eyes. I should have been nervous. I should have been fidgeting or wanting to bite my nails or wanting to hide. But the drinks had taken that away. Instead, the darkness of the room coaxed me to rest as the quiet, faraway music blared up from the kitchen like a lullaby. Sam took a seat next to me and let my head settle on to his shoulder. I could feel his chest rise and fall with each breath, and I wondered if he knew how being this close to him was enough to keep me awake all night—despite the beer and the darkness and the quiet melody from a floor below.

He reached down and held my hand again, and I froze at the feel of it. I wouldn't have moved from that spot if the house were on fire, but he moved us both. He leaned deep back into the cushions and pulled my face to meet his. But instead of smiling at him, I was holding on to him as if he was the center of a merry-go-round and I was sucked into the gravity spin. The alcohol had reached its full effect. I couldn't tell if we were moving clockwise or counter-clockwise, but we were spinning, and I wanted to grip the sides of the couch to keep myself from falling off the edge. He didn't seem to notice. He kissed me once, then twice. I froze.

"You're so pretty." His breath brushed my face.

"I am?" I giggled. It was a strange, airy sound pointed in Sam's direction. It was my mother's laugh, the kind I only ever heard late at night, after her second shift.

"You know you are," Sam answered.

Relief swept over my body. I had confirmation Sam King liked me. He leaned in to kiss me again, but I couldn't move in response. His lips moved against mine, but I laid still in shock.

He pulled back. "What's wrong?"

"Uh ..." I didn't know where to begin. My head was spinning and my stomach was sour. I was desperate to make it stop. But at the same time I couldn't dare move from his arms. He was my first kiss, my first-ever real kiss with a guy. And it wasn't just any first kiss. It was Sam, the one I had dreamt of since I was in seventh grade. I admitted slowly, "I've just wanted ... this ... for a long time."

"Good." He grinned.

"I mean ... like years."

His smile grew and he shook with a silent laugh. I had just given him permission. He pulled me down on to the couch and pressed his lips against mine, and I felt the thickness of his arms and shoulder sweep over mine. Finally, I mustered the courage to kiss him back. But I couldn't keep up. His hand moved quickly along my hips. I tried to break for a breath.

"Sam." I pulled away and felt his cheek against my lips as I spoke.

"It's fine. We're just kissing." He moved his lips across mine sweetly, but he squeezed me closer to him.

Questions shot through my mind like bullets, but they were all moving in slow motion. What did all this mean? I pushed my hands against his chest to create some space, but he didn't budge. He didn't even seem to feel it. If I were to push any harder … if I told him to move … would I ruin my chance?

"We can stop if you want," he whispered.

Just then, there was a cough to my left.

I turned my head and saw that a figure had somehow entered the room without us noticing and taken a seat on the opposite couch. He was hidden by the shadow that extended from the dim light in the hallway.

Sam kissed me again.

Then, another cough.

"Who is that?" I whispered. I squinted my eyes but couldn't make out the shape.

Sam looked up and toward the figure. A look of annoyance registered on his face. "Nobody." He turned my head back toward his lips.

"No, really. There's somebody here. Right in this room."

Sam buried his head into the cushion with a groan of frustration. "What the heck, man?"

The figure didn't respond.

"Get out of here!" Sam yelled.

No response.

"Look, just ignore him," Sam said with an edge of defiance. "He'll go away."

"Huh?" I pushed him off of me and propped myself up on my elbows to get a better view. "Josh?"

"Dang it!" Sam punched the cushion behind me in surrender and pushed himself upright. He stomped out of the room with a huff, leaving me in the room with his best friend.

I pulled my shirt straight and stared at the floor. Why had Josh come into the study with us? I tried to smooth my hair into place, but there was no hope in covering up what I had been doing.

"It's time to go," he said flatly.

"What are you doing in here?" I asked, indignant that he was giving me an order. My chance with Sam was gone thanks to him.

"Sam knows what I'm doing in here, and that's all that matters. Look, the party's over. Let's go." Josh stood and held his hand out to me.

I ignored it. "I came with Julie and JP, not you."

"They've already left, just like almost everybody else. You've been up here for thirty minutes, and I told them I would take you home."

"Julie left?" I stood up slowly, trying my best not to show him that the room was continuing to spin. "Why are you even up here? Did it get boring downstairs?"

Josh snickered. "Something like that."

"I'm not ready to leave." Wherever Sam had gone, I needed to find him and make it right.

"Well, I am. And I'm your only ride back, so you better take it." Josh wasn't giving me an option, and I could see in his eyes that he would embarrass me if I resisted.

I followed him out of the house without saying good-bye to anyone. Humiliation washed over me as I tiptoed down the driveway and settled into the passenger seat of his car.

"Wait here," he commanded. He pulled the seat belt over me and returned to the house alone. Minutes later, he exited, slamming the front door behind him. He took his seat next to me and drove us back toward the island in silence. His body was rigid. The only thing that moved on it was the indention on the side of his jaw as he clenched it in anger.

"I'm not one of those girls, you know."

"You're not?" he replied. "What kind of girl is that?"

"I don't just kiss boys. And I'm not one of those girls who gets herself into situations just to be saved. I was fine back there."

"You were?"

"And why is what I do or how I get home any of your business, anyway?"

No answer.

"Isn't he one of your best friends?"

"That doesn't mean I trust him with you." His dark brows pressed down as he stared at the road ahead of us.

"Well, I can take care of myself," I huffed. The car crossed the humpback bridge on Perico Island, and I felt my stomach lose its bottom. "Oh my gosh, Josh. Pull over. Pull over."

He drove the car to the side of the causeway, and I ran to the mangroves that bordered the marsh. I hunched over and released brown liquid from my stomach. It was the most disgusting thing I'd ever done. And with every convulsion, every time I emptied myself of the alcohol, I could feel a familiar void set in again. The beer had given me courage, the mettle to dance with Sam and let him kiss me, and kiss him back. But reality set in as the beer worked itself out of my system and the old, familiar feelings came back. Josh was going to drive me home to my dark house and empty room, where I would wake up to a mother whose behavior I couldn't predict and a mirror that would tell me I was still alone, that I was still the ugly duckling. I hated that Josh was taking me back there.

There was nothing good about where I was headed, but behind me, even on the sordid couch of Sam King's house, was the first place I ever felt wanted and the first place a boy had ever called me pretty. If I didn't think Josh would disown me as his friend, I would have asked him to take me back.

Josh rubbed my back and helped me back into his car. He seemed unaffected by the spectacle I had just created, though the quiet between us still retained an edge. He turned his headlights off as he pulled into his driveway and helped me to my door in silence.

I turned to meet his stare. "I'm sorry I got sick. Thanks for the ride."

He didn't respond.

Chapter 7

Denise had decided it was going to be a good day, and so we woke up to waffles with syrup and butter. Robby, Crystal, and I stared at each other in silence, not sure if we should trust the happy mother who sang to herself over the morning dishes.

"What's wrong with you three, anyway? You all look like you just saw a ghost. It's Sunday morning. Enjoy your breakfast!" She beamed with a smile from ear to ear at the sight of us.

Robby and I cautiously found our seats.

Crystal didn't waste time and began to pile on the syrup. "Cut it for me, Robby," she ordered.

Robby complied and began to line up the bites in trenches of brown and golden goo.

"You're in a good mood today, Mom." I regretted the remark instantly.

"Of course, I am." The lilt in her voice revealed that I was very close to triggering her defenses.

This is how it is with a woman who rages and convinces herself she's doing it in a vacuum. If I had tried to compare her Sunday morning happy mood to her Saturday morning tantrum, she would have denied such a thing occurred. The dish fell; she didn't throw it down in a fit. She left Ray; he didn't abandon her. She was talking about her ex, not yelling at us kids. And we misheard her, of course. She would never say that *all* men are louses.

I shook the image from my mind and tried to hide the fact that my head was pounding from the night before.

Denise took a seat at the table with us and blew on her cup of coffee. "Is it a crime to be in a good mood or something? It's just a beautiful day. Geez, you're so suspicious all the time."

She was right. Not to mention she was bopping around the house like she was Snow White. I was expecting a little yellow bird to fly in and rest on her shoulder any minute.

"And what's wrong with you, Missy? You look terrible. What were you doing last night?"

The blood rushed to my cheeks. "Now who's suspicious, Mom?"

Robby looked at me as if to let me know he knew better. I'm sure he could smell exactly what I had been up to the night before. Crystal chewed in silence as brown syrup leaked down the side of her chin.

Denise took a seat and pulled her leg under the other. She leaned over the table playfully and turned to Robby. "So, does Bruce own the whole marina or does he have partners?"

And there it was.

"Huh?" Robby replied.

"Well, is he the only boss over there?"

"No, he has a partner too. They both run things," Robby answered begrudgingly. His eyebrows pushed together with tension.

"Well, he seems very connected. He stopped over yesterday to bring you your tips. They're there on the counter, by the way. He sure does run a big operation over there. Did you know they house more than one hundred boats during season? Anyway, I invited him over here for dinner tonight so make sure to clean your room."

Robby stuffed the last bite of waffles into his mouth and pushed himself from the table without saying a word.

I cleaned the table with Crystal, until there was a knock on the door. Julie had come over with her laptop.

"Oh my gosh, get in here!" I grabbed her by the hand and led her to my room, locking the door behind us.

"Before you say anything, Missy, I just want to say I'm so sorry JP and I left you. You were upstairs for so long, and then Josh said that he was going to take you home. But I never should have bailed on you without talking to you first. Forgive me?"

I rolled my eyes. "Yes. Of course."

"So, what were you doing up there?"

I rubbed my lips together as I searched for the words.

Julie couldn't wait any longer. "Let's see ... You weren't with me. You weren't with Josh. But Sam was missing ..."

A loud shriek escaped my lungs at the sound of his name. "He may have been kissing me upstairs."

"No way!"

We sat crisscross on the floor opposite each other as I recounted how Sam invited me, and danced with me, and called me pretty. Not just cute, pretty. I told her every last detail and some I hadn't even remembered until they poured through my blurry recollection.

"So, do you see it now, Missy?" Her bright blue eyes danced underneath a mess of lashes. "You're gorgeous. And everyone sees it. The hottest guy in our class sees it."

I shook my head no. I just couldn't accept it as real.

"And why aren't you ever on Facebook?"

I sighed. "I am. It's just that we don't have a computer here at home so I can never get on. Plus, you've got like five hundred friends, and I don't know anybody here anymore. I'd have five people or something."

Julie powered up her laptop and showed me how to hijack Mrs. Durham's wireless connection. "Just log on and see if he sent anything. I'll bet he's already tried to contact you."

I went to my profile page and looked to see if I had any new friend requests. Zero.

"Whatever." Julie shrugged. "I'm sure he's going to friend you any day. Don't you friend him. You have to play a little hard to get, you know."

She signed on to her account and showed me all the updates from our classmates. JP posted a ping-pong action shot from Friday's party. Leigh complained about not winning at any of the games we played last night. My brother was tagged in a photo skim boarding by the piers. And then the update from Tanya Maldonado:

> Why do some girls think it's hot to get so sloppy?
> People need to go back to 7th grade.

I gasped. Julie shut the laptop and asked what color nail polish I was wearing, but we both knew I had seen the post, and we both knew it was about me. Tanya's update had already received eight comments. The bottom of my stomach dropped again, but I couldn't tell if it was still the effects of last night or the fear of going back to school the next day. There was a whole world already talking about me, and they didn't have to even use my name.

"Who knows who she's talking about." Julie crossed her arms with a grimace.

I peered at her from the top of my eyes. We both knew the answer to that question, and everyone else did too.

"Forget her, Missy."

"How?" I raised my fingers to my mouth and focused on my pointer. Manicure officially ruined.

"Stop biting your nails and forget her. She's just a hater. Sam likes you. Remember *that.* And it doesn't matter if he's friended you or not. If you don't have a chance to talk with him this week, we'll just have to make it happen."

By the time Julie left for the evening, she had left me with a masterful plot to see Sam outside of class again. "It's all about strategic availability," she said. We'd linger after school on Wednesday. She and I both could use the tutoring, and then we could plug ourselves into the stadium stands to watch practice. Sam would be there, running track drills so he could stay in shape for football over the spring. He would see us rooting him on, come over to say hello, and maybe give us a ride home.

I tried to thrust Tanya's comments out of my mind. I wouldn't be sloppy. Instead, I'd be in total control. And Sam would put his arm around me in the bleachers, not because I had too much beer, but because he wanted to pull me closer. *What could she say then?*

I hated that I couldn't shake her comments. And I hated that the greatest victory I could imagine was finding a way for her to forget me altogether. Or, there was the ultimate dream: To become so accepted, so loved, and so popular that it no longer mattered to anyone what she said about me. It was an impossible irony, anyway, of course. If that day ever came and I was still aware of what she was saying about me, I would have already failed.

The sun was on its way to setting into streaks of pink and purple across the sky. Seagulls cried outside my window preparing for their evening hunt. Robby had returned from a day out with his friends and seemed mellowed, now somehow unconcerned with the fact that Denise was closing in on his boss and that his boss would be coming over for dinner. She was baking lasagna, as if deliberately releasing the smell of tomatoes and garlic throughout the house. The scent was warm and inviting, and it made our place seem almost like a normal home.

When Bruce arrived, he gave Robby a playful punch in the arm and took a seat at the head of our kitchen table. His hair was matted to his head from a day of working in the sun, and his round gut swelled beneath his shirt until it stretched the sides around his rib cage. He was burly and bloated, but somehow this made him seem stately. The more space he took up at our table, the more we felt like we needed to listen to him.

Bruce looked Robby in the eyes as he spoke of the boat project underway at the marina. "You're gonna pull in a lot of tips when that boat is ready. A local kid like you will make these old men remember when they were young."

Robby grinned. Maybe I was the only one who feared what would happen now that Denise had inserted herself into Bruce's life.

"You see, it's all about making sure they catch something." Bruce leaned forward, holding his fork and knife in stabbing positions. "You do that, and they'll be emptying out their wallets. And that's what we'll work on, kiddo. We'll work on angling and finding the right spots together so you can lead them directly to the big ones. Then when you take them back to shore, you can take their picture with their catch and charge them for that too. It's a great setup. A real gimme."

Denise scooped another serving of lasagna on to Bruce's plate. "Isn't that so nice of Bruce to do for you, Robby? Showing you the ropes like that?"

"Yep." My brother glared at the kitchen table. Denise had just twisted his after-school job into a charity project.

Bruce's eyes switched between them, my mother vying to be June Cleaver and my brother on the verge of blowing her cover. He coughed to cut the tension. "Nice nothin'. I'm not doin' this kid any favors. He's going to be makin' me money. This isn't no internship, it's work. It's earn your keep. And this kid's a natural."

Robby's shoulders relaxed at his words. I could see the pride in his eyes. He was going to earn this and prove that he could, and I desperately hoped he'd succeed.

"Well," Denise said smartly. "Earning your keep is a lesson he could do to learn. And thank goodness he has you to teach him how."

I shut my eyes at her words. Was she even aware that she had insulted my brother to make Bruce feel like a hero? But neither of them gave her any reaction. The meal was enough distraction to waft offenses out of the room, and the men had already decided exactly what the situation would be. We were going to eat lasagna like a family.

After dinner, Bruce took a seat next to my mother on the couch and twirled her hair in his fingers as we watched television. My mother's face was relaxed for the first time in months, and I was happy for her. Finally.

Would Sam twirl my hair if we were watching TV together? Were his parents finally home? Was he sitting on the couch with them too?

I had to ignore whatever Tanya was saying online. Sam King told me I was pretty. Pretty needed to win out tonight. My mother and I both, I decided, were on our way to getting boyfriends.

• • • • •

When the second-period science teacher walked out of the classroom to attend to a phone call, the class quickly divided into small groups of whispers and chuckles. Cell phones appeared from backpacks and fingers texted wildly to report the play-by-play of the classroom situation.

Julie turned around in her desk with her phone in hand. "I'm so glad we're stuck in this class together. Check out this pic of JP!"

I couldn't help but smile at her. She was smitten. "What's he holding in his hands? Is that our middle school yearbook?"

"He says he's crushed on me for years. He was showing how he drew a heart around my picture when he was like eleven."

We squealed *aww* quietly to each other, barely able to control the thought. Julie had the perfect boyfriend, and she deserved it.

When the classroom chatter dipped, a voice sounded clearly from the back. "She's always been so sloppy." It was just loud enough for Julie and me to hear perfectly.

At the center of a cluster of ponytailed cheerleaders, Tanya Maldonado was pointing her perfectly sloped nose in my direction. Her friends averted their eyes when I found them staring, but Tanya didn't flinch. She stared right back at me with a slight, defiant smile and kept talking, this time so I couldn't hear.

Julie pretended like she didn't see it.

"Are they talking about me?" I could feel my cheeks flush red, the same horrible giveaway that had landed me in trouble with Tanya three years ago. I instinctively began to bite my nails, a habit—I realized for the first time—that allowed me to hide my face with my hand. It didn't matter to Tanya that Sam had invited me. She was talking about me as if I had crashed the party like a cat burglar. She was proof against Julie's belief I could leave the old me behind.

"Who cares?" Julie shrugged.

"I was that bad at Sam's party, huh?"

Julie slouched back in her desk as if to demonstrate how bored she was. "Like she hasn't prayed to the porcelain god herself. That girl isn't all innocent, you know."

Tanya walked to the front of the class to sharpen a pencil and turned toward me. "Hey, Missy." Her voice was like syrup.

"Hi, Tanya," I forced out.

"So, I've been seeing you around lately. You've been hanging out at Sam's."

I nodded. I propped up a friendly smile, hoping to out-nice her out of whatever wickedness she was planning.

Tanya blew the pencil shavings to the floor and walked beside my desk so I had no choice but to look up to her, my neck straining upward. She twirled the pencil in her hand. "I left right about the time you went upstairs. I heard you got *so* wasted and ended up hooking up with Sam. I saw him this morning, and he said he couldn't believe it. He was so drunk. He was so embarrassed."

My voice cracked. "Embarrassed?"

"I mean, he wasn't embarrassed about what he did. Just with who."

I swallowed hard at the shock of her remark.

She stared as if waiting for a response, but I didn't have any to give. By the time she returned to her seat, my eyes had already glassed over with tears that I refused to release.

Julie tried to show me other pictures on her phone, anything to distract me. But it was too late. At the end of class, I gathered my books and headed out as quickly as I could. By the time I arrived at World Civ, I felt like a vacuum had sucked all the air out of my lungs. *Embarrassed.* And not by the fact that he made out with someone but by who he made out with ... I could imagine in full color every possible way Sam was trying to distance himself from me. Using Tanya to do it was about as far away from me as he could get.

I walked into class and kept my eyes on the floor. Sam was already seated behind my desk. He gave a silent nod and quickly looked back to his books. Not even a hello. I waited for him during the lecture to lean into my ear and say something, anything. Crack a joke. Ask for notes. But he sat quietly for the full hour, as if he had no idea I was the same girl who was with him on his parents' couch just two days before. I was invisible.

When the bell rang, and we were released from class, I packed my book-bag slowly. I turned slightly toward the aisle as Sam stood from his desk. Maybe he'd say something to me now that the class was buzzing with other noise.

He threw his bag over his shoulders and stepped around me with care.

"Sorry," I whispered. I tugged my pack out of the aisle.

"No problem," he said. He walked out of the room without looking at me, without even saying my name.

I took the bus home and settled in front of the television, but even Dr. Phil couldn't make me feel better. I was a fool to think this island would be anything different than it always had been. I headed for the cottage.

When I opened the gate, Josh was sitting at the patio table, poring over a book. He looked up at the sound of my arrival.

"I'm sorry. I didn't realize you were here. I can come back another time." I let my hand linger on the handle.

Josh watched, expressionless, for a second too long as I waited for his reaction. "It's fine." He shrugged and turned away. "I'm not staying."

I stood for a moment in the entryway, feeling all over again how I had let him down and at the same time resenting that he had gotten in the way of my time with Sam. I shut the door and approached him.

I walked to the table and waited for him to say something, but no words came. Did he think I was sloppy too? How could he not? He looked my way but didn't look at me, as if he was half asleep.

"Josh, I'm sorry you had to take care of me the other night. Are you mad?"

He shook his head. "No, not at you."

I took a seat and tried to get him to meet my eyes, but he dodged them by staring at the ground below. "Not at me? Then who?"

"No one."

"Well, I can tell you're not okay." I held my breath to brace for his answer. Was he going to ignore me too?

Josh shook his head. "Sam and I had some words. It's over. We're good now." He slammed his book shut. "But it wasn't exactly the best weekend."

"You're mad at Sam? For what?"

Josh curled his hand into a fist. "'Cuz Sam knows better than to give a girl drinks like that and ..."

My mouth dropped open. I understood now why Josh had left the party in such a state. I remembered the door slamming behind him, and how tense he looked on the drive home.

"It wasn't Sam's fault. And I don't need your protection, Josh."

He nodded as if he didn't believe me. "Well, he shouldn't do that to any girl."

"Girls can make up their own minds, you know. It's not his responsibility."

"Guys should hold up the standard, not take advantage when people drop them."

I felt cold at his words.

"I didn't mean it like that, Missy. I just meant that he knew it was your first time in a party like that. He should be looking out for you if you're ... going to be hanging out with him." He finally met my eyes with his own. They were wide and sincere, almost in pain.

I waited for him to say more, to tell me what he really thought of me and how I disappointed him. How he knew Sam was embarrassed to be seen with me.

"Look," Josh said. "Just because a guy likes you doesn't mean that ..." He stopped himself and exhaled.

"What? Are you afraid you're going to insult me?"

Josh's eyes narrowed. "Insult you? No, not you—Sam. Just forget I brought it up."

"Well, it doesn't look like I'm going to be 'hanging out' with Sam, anyway. He doesn't like me. That's pretty clear now. So you don't have to worry about my precious honor."

Josh pursed his lips as if he knew differently. "I guess we'll see about that."

I released my hair from its ponytail and turned to the pool. My last place for peace was quickly becoming a combat zone. Josh began to pack his things, and a short burst of panic escaped in my gut.

"So," I said. "What are you studying, anyway? What's that book?"

"Nothing."

"Please, Josh. Just talk to me."

A small smile eased across his face. "Okay. What do you want to talk about?" He leaned forward, and his shoe brushed against the side of mine underneath the table. He left it there, two centimeters away from my mine. If we were both aware of that space, neither one of us could admit it. And, for a moment, neither of us backed away, as if we were playing chicken to see who'd flinch first. I realized then that I liked being close to him. He wasn't anything like Sam, but every time this boy was in my presence, everything I thought I wanted became a downright blur.

"I want to know what's in that book you're clearly trying to hide from me."

He shifted in his seat as if to brace for my reaction. "All right. You asked, so I'll tell you. I was actually reading a verse in the Bible."

"You were just reading that on your own?"

"Yeah." He forced a small smile, but I could see these words were difficult for him to share.

I didn't know what to say to something like that, but I knew I didn't want to insult him. I looked to the ground as if searching for a script of how to answer.

"I don't mean to be weird," Josh said. "Let's just forget about it."

"No, it's fine. I asked you. So what do your friends say about you reading … that … and not hanging out with them at parties all the time?"

"Friends? You mean like Sam?"

I shrugged.

"They tolerate it. Barely, I guess." Josh shook his head in defeat. "Some of them understand where I'm coming from. Some of them think it's lame, and hate that I've changed. It's hard to explain why

I would be into this. Everything they're doing is right in front of them in that moment. They're answering to no one. And then, here I am, in the middle of it with them, and everything I want to tell them about is invisible to them. But it's just as real, more real, even though I must look crazy."

I had stumbled upon more than just Josh reading a Bible verse. I had walked into the middle of his own personal rebellion. Most of our friends partied and broke their parents' rules. He talked about God and broke his friends' rules.

Josh rolled back his head and moved his foot away. "Let's go swimming, Missy. Isn't that what you're here for?"

"Weren't you getting ready to leave?"

"Well, I've never shown you my one-armed handstand. Obviously, you need to see this, so you have something to aspire to, to practice when I'm not around."

"Aspire to?" I laughed in protest. "I'm Michael Phelps compared to you."

Josh pulled off his shirt and cannonballed into the deep end.

The splash soaked me, and I jumped in behind him. He had sucked the heaviness out of the day in an instant, and I felt free again. We took turns showing off our tricks. He walked upside down on the bottom of the pool, and I somersaulted backward and forward like a mermaid.

A bright, goofy smile spread across his face. "You should try out for the swim team or something."

"Me? I don't think so."

"You actually have mad skills."

I shook my head free from the idea. "Yeah, but it's competitive. I don't think I could do that."

"They'd love you. And you're kind of fun to hang around. You know, when you're sober."

I gasped in shock and splashed him until he swallowed a mouthful of water. Whatever distance he was keeping between us was gone now, erased by the baptism of chlorine and soothed by the palm leaves moving in the now-gathering dusk above.

"Well, Josh, you're not so bad either, when you're not all up in my business."

He laughed knowingly. "Seriously though, Missy. You have an effect on people."

My mouth was suddenly dry. I feathered my arms backward and forward to stay afloat. "I have an effect on people? I've never heard it put like that before." I thought about the effect I seemed to have on people like Tanya Maldonado. Immediate and visceral, it always seemed.

"I see you with your sister sometimes. You love her a lot. You always take care of her and try to keep her protected." He backed himself against the side of the pool. "And your brother too. You're always keeping an eye out for him, even though he's older than you."

Embarrassment began to cover over me like a veil. These seemed to be good things. But there had to be something else lurking. What else did he see? I remembered all the drama he had watched play out on my front yard. This was pity talk. "Thanks, Josh. But you don't have to say all that."

He blinked, and his eyes focused on me like he was willing me to believe him.

I had liked Sam King since I was in seventh grade, and I had never been closer to getting him to look my way, even if he didn't talk to me in class. But I couldn't deny something had connected between us at the party. Maybe it wasn't over. Maybe he didn't say those things that Tanya said.

But whenever I was around Josh, something about Sam seemed to fade just a bit. I found myself answering strange questions, like how many centimeters were between our feet and how many times he looked me in the eyes.

Josh had every opportunity to kiss me, to hold my hand, to ask me on a date, to show me that somehow I was more to him than just a neighbor and to tell me that I shouldn't be going after Sam King. But he had done nothing. Not when he caught me in his grandmother's pool. Not when he gave me the key to the cottage. Not when he took me home from parties on long drives back to the island. He never made a single move, as if invisible shackles bound him from pursuing anything beyond friendship.

The water danced between us, and we held on to the side of the pool for support. I could feel the currents from his kicks ripple around my waist.

I dare you, Josh Durham.

He inhaled deeply, and I wondered if he was going to call my bluff. "So, your brother Robby is a pretty good skimmer. Do you skim too?"

I shut my eyes in frustration. "No, I don't skim. That's a Robby thing."

"Oh," he answered.

I knew I couldn't hold it against him. I couldn't blame him, either. How could Josh want to date me after he had just peeled me off of one of his best friends' couch?

He pushed himself out of the pool and sat on the edge with his legs dangling in. The water rushed off of his shoulders and formed a puddle around him. "So, what are you doing Wednesday after school?"

"Wednesday?" I searched for words. That was the day Julie and I were going to watch Sam's practice after school.

"Yeah, come hang out with me."

One side of my mouth began to tug upward. "Where?"

"Does it matter? You'll be with me."

I pretended to think hard and rolled my eyes up to the side.

"It's a get-together with my church group."

Oh. Not a date. "Uh," I stalled.

"What? You afraid?"

I placed my hands on my hips to show I was not interested in his game, but it didn't help my case. His white teeth glimmered in the twilight. He was beautiful in his own dark, unpredictable way, and it made me surrender my disinterest. "Afraid? Maybe. What are they serving? Kool-Aid?"

"Nah, just young virgins."

A smile broke across my face.

"A bunch of kids from our school and some from other schools will be there. You can bring Julie and JP, whoever."

Definitely not a date. "Thanks, but no. I'm actually hanging out with Julie that day. We already arranged it." I couldn't give up on the plan Julie and I had hatched to see Sam outside of class, not when there was still a chance and not when Josh just seemed to view me as one of his church charity projects.

"That's fine. So, what are you guys doing anyway?"

"Um, well, straight after school we're going to a math tutor."

He squinted his eyes as water streamed from his hair and down his face. "Well that lasts an hour. What about after?"

"After tutoring?" I drew out the seconds. "Julie and I were going to hang out. Maybe watch practice."

His eyes narrowed. "Track practice?"

"Yeah," I answered a little too bubbly.

He sat up just enough for me to notice. "You gonna cheer on Sam?"

I looked down to the water in embarrassment. "I don't know. I mean, why not?"

He snickered to himself and shook his head as if to push the idea out of his mind. "There's no why not. Have fun."

"I mean, maybe next time . . ."

"No. It's fine. Have fun."

Josh pushed himself to his feet and gathered his books. He threw the towel around his neck, grabbed his shirt, and said good-bye without making eye contact. "Sorry, I just remembered I need to get home early tonight. My grandma's back, and she's got dinner for me. I'll catch you later."

He disappeared into the thick trees around the property and left me to swim alone. I wondered what he'd tell his grandma when he came back in swim trunks and a towel, with no bodysuit or skim board; I couldn't lose this cottage pool, and I had to trust he didn't want to either.

On Wednesday morning, Robby and I were both stuck riding the bus. Ricky Brewer had ditched my brother that morning. It seemed like every other upperclassman on the entire island had found a ride to school, except for us. We were still sentenced to the yellow school bus that would take us over two bridges to the mainland. It was a long way to ride in a vehicle with Tanya Maldonado, who surely was managing her own embarrassment at the situation by holding court at the back of the bus. How could a girl who dated college boys be sentenced to ride on a bus for thirty minutes every morning? It was a great injustice even I couldn't understand.

"Messy," I thought I heard her say. The next time, it was clearly Missy. It was the only word I could work out in a roar of whispers from the back seat. Tanya was convening a conference again, and this time it was with a gang of eager freshmen who might as well have been sitting around her feet. It was as if she was grooming the next generation of smug, popular kids to taunt the next generation of kids like me.

One of them jumped seats to sit across the aisle from me. "Psst," he said.

I turned in my seat to see his green eyes wide with mischief.

"Missy, you doing anything tomorrow night? I have some beer. Maybe we could hang out?"

"What?" I questioned, hoping to play dumb.

"Yeah, you like to party, right?" His bony knees inched closer to me as he tried to look down my shirt. Snickers erupted from the back as he leered at my chest.

I looked to the back, where Tanya pretended not to be paying attention. I could see the game of telephone now. She held court with a few chosen freshmen, told them how trashy I was, and this kid had to do nothing but take the bait. If he got a rise out of me, it might impress her. It was like a gossip relay race.

"So," the kid pressed. "You up for it, hottie?"

"I don't know what you're talking about." I sank deep into my seat, hoping to hide my head from Tanya's line of view.

Suddenly, Robby turned around from the seat in front and grabbed the kid by the collar. "What are you saying to my sister, you little punk?" His teeth clenched in anger, and I could see he was just seconds away from clobbering the boy.

"What, man? Nothing. Nothing. Forget about it." The freshman waved his arms in mock surrender, pretending to turn my brother's warning into a joke. But Robby wasn't joking, and he outweighed the kid by at least thirty pounds. The boy settled back in his seat as his face grew red.

"It's okay, Robby," I whispered. I placed my hand on his shoulder to calm him. I was grateful for what he did, but I couldn't stand it if he got expelled. He'd come close a few times already this year.

"No, it's not okay." He gritted his teeth, barely containing his rage. "I may be a sack of nothing, but you are not."

"What?" I said, my voice cracking.

"Never mind. But no one gets to talk to you that way." He pushed himself to the window and closed his eyes. In a few seconds he was asleep, and I had to shake him to get off the bus for school.

Chapter 8

If I was going to incur the wrath of Tanya Maldonado again, I was at least going to know if Sam truly had no real interest in me.

After the last period, a hornet's nest of students zipped and bumped around the hallways in a frenzy of T-shirts and bubble gum. Julie found me hiding by my locker and nodded in a sharp show of resolution. "Tutoring. Bleachers. Boom."

I squinted my eyes in disbelief. "Boom?"

"Boom," she repeated matter-of-factly. "He's going to see you up there, and he's going to realize how much he likes you, and that will be the end of the story. Boom."

I bit my lip, unsure.

"You *do* still like him, right?"

My stomach tightened into a cramp. "More than I should."

"Well, let's get it done."

"Julie, this is beginning to feel like a movie where the guy just isn't that into you. Sam's had three days to talk to me in class, and he's practically gone out of his way to ignore me. Maybe Tanya was telling the truth."

Julie shook her head to silence me. "There's only one way to find out."

Right. But I wasn't sure I wanted to know. When tutoring was over, we plowed our way to the field, applied a new coat of lip gloss, and headed up the bleachers. They rattled with each of our steps as if to announce that I was now, officially, "conveniently available" for Sam to notice me.

We watched the players sprint and stretch and time themselves. The sun was blazing on the black asphalt, and I did my best not to stare at Sam too long.

"Oh!" Julie elbowed me in the side. "He just looked up here at you. Did you see that?"

"This is a stupid idea. We should go." I rocked my foot back and forth over crossed legs. I didn't want to know if he looked up at me. If he looked and didn't come to say hello, it would be worse than not looking at all.

"Just wait. They're wrapping up now. He's obviously going to come up here to say good-bye or will wave or something."

I turned to Julie. "Have I told you what a great friend you are? No one else would sit out here with me like this. Pretty desperate."

"Not desperate. Strategic."

We sunk into the bleachers and laughed extra loud in the hope that our giggles would carry down to the field. I hated being a girl sometimes.

Finally, the coach blew a whistle to end practice and Sam headed to the bench to take a drink of water. He wiped the sweat off his forehead and tilted his head back to swallow a large gulp. He was looking right at me.

"There," Julie whispered through gritted teeth.

I held my breath and Sam's eyes. Boys milled around him, grabbing drinks, wiping themselves off with towels, and creating a jumble of what could only be crude jokes and insults. Sam rubbed the side of his neck and then, with nothing more than a slow blink, he turned away. He followed the team into the locker room and didn't give me another look.

Julie and I sat in silence as seagulls called in the distance. Were they lost, flying around so far into town? I couldn't get back to the island fast enough.

"Don't worry about it." I raised my palm in a show of surrender. "I mean, whatever. He doesn't have to like me. It's not the end of the world."

Julie eyes filled with sympathy, and I had to glance away.

"Look, let's not talk about it. It's over."

She nodded as if trying to convince herself. "Okay. Well, we're just going to have to forget about it by having a lot of fun next weekend."

I choked out a laugh. "Next week?"

"Yeah, in just over a week, Club B is opening. JP wants to take us there." She rolled her neck with an attitude. "So get excited."

• • • • •

"Are you smoking now?" I planted my hands on my hips.

Robby didn't answer. His headphones blared over his eardrums. It was nearing nine o' clock that night, and JP and Julie were already late to pick me up to take me to my first dance club. It had been two weeks since Sam kissed me on his parents' couch, and I had nothing better to distract me from counting the days than harassing my brother.

"Why are you hanging out with those losers?" I couldn't keep the bossy tone out of my voice.

He pulled off the headphones and looked at me with half-dazed eyes. "Huh?"

I sat on his bed and wiggled around until he huffed loudly in exasperation. Crystal snuck into the room and crawled on my lap. It would be impossible to resist the two of us.

"I'm sorry I haven't been around much," he mumbled. "I've been busy with the boat and then hanging out with my friends. You know."

I leaned my head against the glass panes of his makeshift bedroom wall and studied his pencil drawings taped above the dresser. Robby pulled a sketchpad close to his chest as if to hide it from our prying eyes.

"What is that?" Crystal peeked over.

"Nothing."

"Show me!"

She tried to pry the pad away by tickling him.

"What do you guys want?" He whined, but a smile gave way.

"What are you drawing this time?" she pressed.

I smiled at the sight of them. It was pointless to fight her, and we both knew it. He finally lowered the paper. It was a sketch of a boat, his boat, looking bright and well-ordered in the bay.

"Is that the boat you're working on?" I asked.

He shrugged his shoulders, like admitting it would make it all disappear.

"It's really good! You did all that with a pencil?"

"It's all right." Robby nodded reluctantly. "I'm still trying to get the hang of making the water look real."

"It's beautiful!" Crystal touched the edge of the paper with awe.

It was good. My brother was a genius with art and his bedroom walls offered proof of it. They were papered with pictures of girls from the neighborhood and surfers and fantasy creatures that he somehow made look real.

I leaned over his shoulder. "And what's that figure at the bottom of the picture? Is that your signature or something?"

I pointed to two letters:

R̃K

Robby popped his knuckles to stall. "Kind of. So, the initials are my initials. But the wavy line on top is a symbol for water. It comes from one of the Native American tribes. I found it online."

I studied my brother's cryptic signature.

Robby's eyes widened as he explained. "Yeah, well, you know how our dad was part Cherokee and we're like one-fifth Cherokee or whatever? I mean, it's like the only thing I really know about him, where we come from on that side. And I love the water so much. So I just wanted to make it part of the way I sign things. Like my stamp."

It was just a line in the pattern of a wave. Simple and rudimentary, and yet my brother had found a way to make it look elegant and strong. The symbol hung over his initials and cast a shadow on the brightness of the letters below, not much unlike our father, a mysterious, dark question that would hang over us for the rest of our lives. But together, the initials and the symbol were beautiful. Robby was holding on to some small part of who we were, which was all we knew. It didn't matter to me if the Internet was right or not about that symbol. It mattered that he was trying to hold on.

Goosebumps formed on my forearm as I saw my brother's passion for his art and his boat and the way he signed his name. "It's really great, Robby."

He stood up from his bed and found a soccer ball to kick between his feet. He was done talking about himself. "So, where are you headed tonight?"

"JP and Julie are taking me to Club B."

He laughed wildly. "You're kidding, right?"

"No."

He shook his head. "Well, you shouldn't be worried about me. I should be worried about you. That place is a hole."

I crossed my arms. "Whatever. It's just a club."

"Yeah, in Bradenton. How cool can it be? It's just gonna be a bunch of other kids from other schools looking for some rock star experience. And everyone'll look all mysterious and wild for about a half second, until you get up close and you see that they're just like you. Because, oh yeah, we're in a teen club in Bradenton."

I threw a pillow at his head. "You're such a hater. It sounds good enough for me! Not everyone can be too cool to be bothered like you."

He shrugged. "Yeah. I'll probably be there next weekend."

The thought of new kids was actually a relief, considering the two weeks of high school purgatory I had survived since Sam's party. At least no one at Club B would know they were supposed to ignore me or laugh at me.

"I'm just going to check it out." I raised my hands as if pleading surrender.

Robby smirked. "Well, I don't see why you're going to go hang out there, when you could be hanging out with Josh. I know he's not going to be there."

Crystal jumped with excitement at our next-door neighbor's name.

"With Josh?" I squinted my eyes in confusion.

Robby pointed his finger in little circles toward me. "I'm just sayin'."

I gasped at his insinuation. "Ugh. You're so weird. I'm leaving now."

I shrugged the comment off as Robby laughed dramatically in the background. I forced myself to wait in the living room, where Denise was snuggling up with Bruce on the couch.

Julie had convinced me that I could have a good time by going out dancing, and everyone knows best friends are rarely wrong about that kind of thing. I could forget Tanya. And how Sam ignored me. And how I disappointed Josh, who never made a real move anyway. I could also test out the theory I so much wanted to believe, that I had really blossomed like Julie said. At Club B, no one would know me.

The *B* was for Bradenton, we presumed, but to Julie and me it meant boys. To the club owners, it meant an opportunity to charge every kid under the age of twenty-one a five-dollar cover charge to drink two-dollar Cokes, which by the end of the night would add up to more money than most of us could afford to spend. The idea was straightforward: Give high school and junior college kids the opportunity to go to a club while they were still underage. Decorate the inside with cheap plastic, turn the lights low, and pump the music so loud their heads threaten to explode from excitement. Needless to say, every girl I knew was prohibited from going, including Julie. And this is why she planned to stay the night at my house. Denise wouldn't notice when we snuck in late.

"I don't recognize most of these people," Julie whispered to me as we waited in line.

Leigh and a few of her other friends ran up alongside of us, each of them underdressed for the cool, late February air. "It's gonna be hot inside. I left my sweater in the car," she explained. "Check it out. Everyone here must go to other schools. I can tell by those girls' eyeliner they're not from in town."

Julie laughed. "Be quiet. They might hear you."

I had been looking forward to spending a night with a crowd who wouldn't know me from school. But once I saw their strange faces, all I wanted to do was find my own group and stay with them.

The bouncer, who looked like a former offensive lineman, stamped the top of our hands and ushered us inside, where loud booms of bass pulsated from the speakers in every corner of the club. Julie, Leigh, and I headed to the dance floor as JP stayed near the bar with the guys. Within moments, more and more people rushed on to the floor, and it was clear the air conditioner couldn't keep up with the heat coming off of us as we raised our arms to the beat.

Boys we didn't know surrounded us. Sweat flowed down their foreheads and through their shirts until the whole dance floor began to look more like gym class than a nightclub. Soon, the sweat became a badge of honor, because it meant we were dancing hard and out after midnight and probably talking to someone from a rival school.

As Julie and I bounced to the music, a boy in a baseball cap made his way to my side. He danced close to me until I finally looked his way. And when I made eye contact, he closed in.

I smiled. He smiled. And our two groups were suddenly bonded, as if we had known each other for years. It was intoxicating. I noticed JP quickly moved to Julie's side before she gathered too much attention from a few of the guys.

When I finally looked up, I saw Sam staring at me from the far side of the room. He was flanked by his usual crew, but he wasn't dancing with them. His mouth was slightly open and his eyes were focused intently. He was watching me.

JP stepped in front of me and blocked my view. "All right, Lady Gaga. I think we all need to go home now." He led Julie and me out of the club and back to his truck.

"I have never seen you like that before!" Julie squealed. "I mean, you were like totally hot out there, and that guy was all about you!"

I laughed at the strange feeling of being okay with attention. "No, he wasn't."

"He was entranced! And don't think I didn't see Sam on the other side of the club. He got there right at the end, and he froze the second he saw you."

My cheeks flushed with heat. "I've never even been dancing before."

Julie giggled. "Trust me, no one could tell. You owned it! And that guy was so cute!"

JP mimicked her and started the ignition with a pout. "That guy was so cute!"

Julie kissed him on the cheek and turned to me to explain. "JP wasn't a big fan."

"That place was lame," he grunted. "It was fine if you like other guys looking at your girlfriend. That one dude was lucky I didn't take him outside."

Julie and I rolled our eyes, but inside a pain hit me in the chest. What would it be like to have a boy who cared about me, who would actually be willing to fight for me? If I couldn't have it for real, maybe going out was a fair substitution. At night, it seemed, I could be right in the center of everything. I could become someone else. I could escape to where there would be guys who would like me and not be afraid to show it, because they didn't know me. When the sun went down, I could get a fresh start.

Julie and I snuck back into my house and settled in for sleep. I pulled my hair away from my neck and settled into the warmth of the pillow. As I inhaled, my breath collected in short, anxious spurts. Some voice inside me wouldn't let me sleep in peace. I wasn't enough to be loved in the daylight, no matter what plan I made.

• • • • •

Monday in World Civ, I steeled myself for Sam King ignoring me again. I took my seat long before he arrived to class, and when he finally walked down the aisle to sit behind me, I saw his face pointed toward me in my periphery. I couldn't resist looking up. I met his eyes. He winked.

At the end of the day, I walked by the stadium to catch the bus back to the island. I heard a voice shout from behind me, "Missy!"

I looked out of the corner of my eyes. *Sam?*

"Missy, wait up! Dang, you're fast!"

I stopped in my tracks when other kids started to look, and turned around to find Sam running to catch up with me. His dark navy shirt enhanced his eyes, and I couldn't help but smile that I had winded a football star.

"Hey." I shifted the books in my arms to the side and felt the eyes of every person boarding the bus for the island stare at the back of my head.

"Hey, yourself." He sucked in a few deep breaths and put his hands on the top of his legs as if to rest. "I've been trying to catch up with you from the other side of the campus. You're pretty quick, you know?"

I nodded, afraid to look too eager to talk to him.

"So, listen, I was wondering if I could give you a ride home."

"A ride. Really?" *Maybe Tanya put him up to this.* "The island's not anywhere near you."

He scratched the top of his wheat-colored hair and squinted into the sun. "Exactly."

Tanya Maldonado walked by us toward the bus. As she passed, her mouth dropped open just enough for me to notice. She didn't speak to Sam. She didn't take her eyes off of me.

A wash of satisfaction wiped the distrust from my face. "Sure. You can give me a ride home," I said extra loud.

Sam blinked. "Okay, then. It's a date."

I laughed. "A date?"

"Well, if I take you to get a shake it's a date."

I caught my breath at the shock of the word. He was asking me out. Proper. In the daylight. "Okay." I could barely force out the word. *Recover yourself, Missy.* "I'd love to, but can I get a fudge shake?"

"Is there any other kind?" He took the books from my arms and walked me to his SUV. When he opened the door for me to get into the passenger side, I tried not to look too impressed, as if this sort of thing happened to me every day.

When we arrived at the ice cream shop, we took seats on the outdoor deck. A server plopped fudge milk shakes in front of us with spoons stuck in the center. The smell of grease and cheeseburgers floated from her apron as she turned back toward her small kitchen.

Sam tilted his head. "I'm sorry I haven't been around. I've been busy."

"Busy. Really?"

He shrugged. "Kind of."

I could only stare as cars raced down the main avenue, blowing wind over the deck as they passed with the sound of a whoosh.

"Look, I've been acting stupid, and I'm sorry. I hope you're not mad at me. You've changed a lot since the old days. Like a lot ..." He stopped himself there as if he was about to insult me. "And I saw you out this weekend, and, well, you know you're hot." The dimples appeared again. His greatest weapon.

"I'm not mad."

"Good."

There was no discussion of the last two weeks. There was no explanation for why he seemed to ignore me in World Civ. There were no hard questions about whether he was embarrassed he made out with me, like Tanya had said. There was none of that because I didn't ask. Sam reached across the table to take my hand in his. It was a real date, it was my first, and I wasn't going to ruin it.

When I arrived at World Civ the next day, the class fell to a sudden hush as I entered the room. I sucked in my belly, pushed my hair to the side in my best effort to look pretty, and tried to fight the nervous smile that was puckering my lips. Ian and Mike didn't even try to fight staring at me as I made my way down the aisle.

"You look gorgeous today, Missy." Sam tugged at my skirt as I tried to take my seat in front of him. "Come here."

"What?" I laughed soft and nervous.

"Come here." He squinted up toward me like I was the sun and pulled on my hand until I fell onto his lap. He wrapped his arms around me like a bear. And in one movement, the question as to whether he was going to bring "us" into public was answered. The class came to a standstill. And Ian and Mike were left to do nothing but nod with approval.

I could barely breathe at the spectacle I had become. Everyone was looking at me, which was normally the worst thing that could ever happen. But with Sam's chin buried into my shoulder, I was safe. He had given me immunity.

I took my seat before Mr. Miller could object to the scene we had created. Sam twirled my hair from behind as I pretended to take notes, giggles wanting to burst from inside me. And I, Melissa Anne Keiser, swooned.

After class, Sam walked me to lunch, holding my hand. Ponytails whipped to the side. Boys stopped messing around mid-smack. The school stopped moving, it seemed, to watch Sam King hold my hand. Once Julie saw this, we'd have to plan a sleepover just to break it down in all its gooey details.

In my mind, there are few things more important to a new relationship than the first time a guy holds your hand in public. First dates and first kisses are important moments, flittering about in some cloud of over-rehearsed manners and expectations. But the first time a guy holds your hand in front of his friends is a statement. There's no purpose to it, no function. It exists for one reason only. And in eleventh grade, just two months before prom, it is an act of revolution.

Tanya Maldonado knew it. She stopped mid-chew as I strolled hand-in-hand with Sam to the lunchroom table where she sat. No one exchanged glances of shock and disbelief with her as I walked with impunity through the lunchroom. They weren't looking at her at all. They were looking at me, and I was beaming.

"Make a seat for Missy, everybody," Sam said.

Tanya was the last to move over, but she did. And the two of us entered into an unspoken treaty. Make that a cold war.

From that point on, it didn't matter who was at the table or what they said to me in the seventh grade. It didn't matter if I sat next to Tanya or Ian or anyone else who remembered calling me Messy. So long as I could feel Sam's long arm around my shoulders, they were friendly, and I was at rest. I had the power to wave Julie over to our booth and bring her into Sam's inner circle. I had opinions people wanted to hear. I had music mixes people wanted to borrow. Being next to Sam was like tagging base. I was safe so long as I could stay there.

Josh sat just a few seats away, close to us, but with nothing much to say. He pushed his food to the side, clenched his jaw, and talked to everyone in the low, quiet voice that I had come to know across the cottage pool, the pool that no one at the table knew anything about but us.

Chapter 9

JP, get your fishing pole off that gator!" Julie covered her eyes with her hands. "I can't even watch you! I can't bear to look!"

JP laughed mischievously and cast his line until a feathery lure dropped on to the alligator's snout. He reeled it in before the beast had a chance to respond.

"Please, stop doing that." Julie brought her hand down as her eyes filled with tears. "It's too scary. He's going to jump into this boat and get us all."

"Don't be ridiculous. He's more afraid of us than we are of him." JP turned to Julie with a know-it-all smirk and then exhaled in surrender at the sight of her trembling lips. "Fine, I'll quit playing."

Julie's shoulders dropped in relief. We had convinced JP we were capable of being proper redneck girls for a day, but we broke that act the second we saw our first alligator. The two-hour drive to JP's family cabin brought us to the center of the state, where a bass boat had been left unguarded and the lake too full of stock to remain unfished. Such a thing was against Florida religion.

Sam rummaged through a tackle box in search of a new hook, and my brother snaked iced tea through his teeth, shooting it across the black, flat water that stretched before us into swamp. The novelty of going fishing with the boys had ended within the first hour. Julie and I rolled our eyes in a consolidated show of boredom.

JP drove the boat several yards away from the gators and let it float freely in the invisible current that rose from underwater springs. "It's cool to hang out with you, Robby. We never see you around. I haven't really gotten to spend time with you since middle school, man."

Robby nodded. I could tell he liked JP, which is why he agreed to come, but Sam was a different story. He had not said more than a few words to my almost boyfriend all day. Neither had I for that matter. Sam seemed perfectly contented on the lake with his fishing gear. He left me to bait my own hook, and I wondered if I was anything more than an annoyance to him. The five of us were an unlikely crew, and my brother the most unlikely member of all.

The sun beat upon us relentlessly as Julie and I leaned across the back of the boat and tried to count the gators in the far distance. Their eyes popped up from the water like slime-colored golf balls.

"The number of inches between their eyes is how many feet they are long." Sam cast his line toward the high grass.

I squinted to evaluate. "Well, in that case, we're looking at some six- and seven-footers." Shivers ran down my spine. There was nothing to keep one from jumping up on to our boat. I'd seen plenty of those shows on cable television.

Robby wedged himself between Julie and me and whispered, "This is how every teen horror movie starts. The gators go after the virgins."

"Get away!" We screamed in unison and slapped him so hard we left red welts on his back. Sam and JP chuckled.

As the afternoon passed and the sun continued its assault, the tops of our arms turned a brownish-red. Julie tapped her feet with impatience. "Let's go back to the cabin and get some drinks or something. I need to get off this boat."

JP turned to her in confusion. "But we haven't caught anything yet."

"Exactly. And we've been out here all day. *And* it's hot out here."

"Well, jump in for a dip."

Julie crossed her arms and looked at her boyfriend with narrowed eyes. "Very funny."

"Fine." JP started the engine, and the boys pulled in their fishing poles. We zipped across the lake at full speed. The wind whizzed by us and water sprayed from the side of our boat on to our skin. At the end of a long canal, we docked at a convenience store and headed inside for snacks. Julie and I stuck our heads in the freezer to relieve our sunburns and pulled ice cream cones from the shelves.

It wasn't long before Sam spotted a volleyball court at the side of the store. "Let's play."

Three other boys joined them for a match, and Julie and I watched from underneath the shade of an orange tree. We laid our towels beneath the branches and watched for red ants.

"Isn't this great?" Julie sighed. She rested her head on my shoulder.

"What's that?"

"We're here with our *boyfriends*."

"Shh. He might hear you." We giggled at the thought and tried to concentrate on the volleyball game. I also tried not to read too much into what Julie had just said—because all day I'd wondered if this trip was proof Sam and I were actually together.

Sam was a natural at the game, as was JP. But I knew my brother hadn't played in years. His athletic ability began and ended at surfing, and there were no waves this far into the mainland. He missed one shot. Then the next.

"Come on, man." Sam bumped Robby with his shoulder after the other team scored a point. "Spike it next time."

Robby couldn't keep up. JP couldn't help him. And Sam wasn't willing to lose.

The other team served the ball over the net, and it shot like a bullet right to my brother's thin arms. Sam stepped in front of him and volleyed the ball to JP to prevent Robby from missing.

"I had that," Robby said.

"Sure you did." Sam stretched out his neck and walked back to his position.

"I did." My brother walked toward him, and the two stared each other down like pit bulls in a caged fight.

JP stepped between them. "Match is over, guys. Come on."

Sam tilted his head to the side. "It's over because we lost."

Julie put her hand on my arm as we held our breath and watched.

Robby wasn't as big as Sam, but he wasn't a coward. He stepped forward, smirked, clenched his fist, and then, as if he was suddenly overcome with exhaustion or a total lack of interest, he rubbed his chin and nodded. "Yeah. Actually, we probably could've won without me getting in your way."

Tension fled from my shoulders. My brother, the peacemaker.

Sam offered a thin smile. "No, I doubt that. I sucked today." He turned to look at me for an explanation, but I knew there wasn't one.

This is why half the surfers on the island worshiped Robby and half the teachers couldn't stand him. He kept us all on edge.

My brother wiped his forehead of sweat and complained of the heat. "Dang, that lake looks good." Before I understood what he meant, he was running toward the docks.

"Where is he going?" Julie asked.

His legs pumped hard as he darted over the long, wooden pier. He showed no signs of slowing down when he neared the edge. The dock didn't end in the middle of the lake, where the vast expanse could offer a reasonable swim. We were by the edge, where the high grass and mud formed a barrier to the water. Signs were posted in the banks: NO SWIMMING: ALLIGATORS

I rose from the towel and raced down the dock after him. "Robby, don't!"

JP, Sam, and Julie followed me. By the time we reached the water's edge, my brother was up to his neck in the murky water.

He lay on his back and kicked his feet wildly. "Feels good!"

"Man, you're crazy!" JP stood on the rim of the dock's last wooden plank and wiped the back of his neck as if trying to relax himself. "Do you know what's in the water around here? This is a breeding area."

Sam laughed. "Dang! You have a death wish or something?"

I pulled on JP's shirt. "Please, go get the boat and pick him up. Please, JP, quickly."

I couldn't understand my brother. There was no moderation. He was either over the top or checked out. It was this kind of stuff that held him back in school in the first place. By the time we pulled him to the boat deck, my brother had spent his energy, and we were left to drive to Anna Maria in silence.

It was nightfall, and the streets of the island were dark except for the blue glow of televisions through the windows. Sam dropped off JP and Julie and let Robby out in the driveway in front of our home. He leaned across me and locked the passenger door. The look in his eyes told me he wasn't going to let me go without a fight.

"Don't go inside."

I smiled. "What do you want to do?"

"Anything. With you."

I blushed and felt my sunburnt cheeks grow hot. "Well, it's late, and my place isn't exactly an option." I saw Bruce's SUV in our driveway. Somewhere inside my mother was playing house with a man who just might be the best one she ever dated. I smiled at the thought. Was she making him dinner tonight?

"Well, you're the island girl. I live in town, so you'll have to tell me where we can go."

I knew exactly where I could take him. "Wait here." I directed him to park out of sight on a neighboring street. I ran to my house, grabbed the key, and returned to his SUV.

"You look like you're up to trouble," he said.

"Is that so?" I looked around to make sure no one was watching.

Sam grinned and took my hand. I led him through the thick grass and past the shrubs and palms of my backyard, then Josh's.

"Are we visiting Josh?" he asked a little too loudly.

"No," I whispered. "And be quiet."

We continued through thick trees and on through the gate of the cottage's backyard, where the pool was still and lifeless. Somewhere in the distance, a streetlight reflected through the trees and on to the water, and I imagined for a moment it was the moon.

"This is perfect." Sam didn't ask how I came to know about it or whose house it was, and I didn't offer. But the knowledge of it weighed heavy on my mind.

I walked the perimeter of the pool and listened to ensure no one was close by. "So, you seen Josh much lately? I haven't seen him in a while." I was curious.

"No. His head's been somewhere else lately. Whatever."

"What do you mean?"

"It's nothing," Sam said flatly. "He'll get over it." He pulled off his shirt and jumped into the water with a giant splash. "Yahoo!"

A neighbor's dog barked, and the noise echoed through the trees. I waved my arms wildly to stop him.

"What's wrong, Missy?" He feigned innocence. "Are we not supposed to be here?"

I raised a finger to my mouth for silence. "Just shut up."

I could tell Sam was tired of talking, even though he had only said a few sentences to me all day. He tilted his head to the side and smiled bashfully. "Okay, we'll be quiet then." He swam to the edge and reached for my ankle. "You're beautiful."

Beautiful.

I revealed my bathing suit and took a seat on the side of the pool to let my legs paint circles in the water. In the weeks since Sam first held my hand at school, he had invited me to parties and taken me to a movie. But we had never been this alone. And he had never told me what he meant by it, by any of it. I had no idea if he was dating someone else, or what he meant by inviting me out, sitting with me at lunch, allowing me to tag along in his harem of friends, and then not calling me for a few days at a time. He hadn't asked me a single question since I had known him. And he hadn't asked me to prom.

Yet every time I saw him, I flushed from the thought that he would even look my way. If I could go back and visit seventh-grade me, she would never believe it. Not in a million years. I wanted to be closer to him. I wanted his attention—to have his eyes on me, and not on any of the million distractions that crossed his path in the halls every day.

This is why they call it a crush. I wanted it to be love so bad that it made my stomach hurt.

Sam pulled me off the edge and into the water. The heavy smell of the lake had washed off him, and I could detect only the clean, bright scent of chlorine and a hint of grass just outside the pool. I noticed his eyes were tired from a day in the sun, and then he shut them and leaned in for a kiss. Warm lips pressed against mine with a sense of determination.

Finally, I had his attention.

He was focused and eager, not waiting for me to kiss him back.

I pulled back to catch my breath. *What was he thinking? What did he think of me?*

He smiled and pressed his forehead against mine. "It's fine."

I nodded.

He kissed me again and pulled me close to him. It felt good to be in his arms, to have his focus on me. I suddenly felt like a caged bird flapping my wings in excitement. But in the water I had no leverage, weightless and in his arms. I pulled back, just enough to keep my bearings, but he ignored me and pressed harder.

How I wanted to believe he was everything I imagined all these years, and now I finally had the opportunity to see for myself. I wanted desperately to be what he wanted, a girlfriend he could be proud of. And wasn't he a good guy? Didn't he open doors for me? Didn't he tolerate my rogue brother? For me?

He was. He did.

I wanted him to see me, really see me. I wanted to know why he spent time with me and why I couldn't shake the feeling I was a prop, a sideshow act on the way to some greater destination he had mapped out in front of him. I had been on his arm at least a dozen times, but I couldn't tell you how many times he had looked into my eyes or how many things about my family he knew. How could he really like me, how could he ever feel the same way I felt, if he didn't know me? How could I trust my own feelings when I didn't really know him either? But these things seemed insignificant when he kissed me.

The next question was as vulgar as it was honest: How far was I going to go to be the center of his world? And wasn't the fact that I even asked myself this question a sign that I might be an even greater manipulator than he had ever thought to be?

I pushed his hands away gently. "Sam, take it easy."

"Come on. You didn't act all uptight at my party. I didn't know you were like this."

I felt the breath leave my lungs at the implication. "What?"

He didn't have a chance to answer.

A voice weathered by age shouted from behind. "Who is in there?" I could see her cutting her way across the yard with a flashlight until she reached the edge of the water. "Who's in my pool?"

Sam and I froze in fear. It was too late to get out of the water and make a run for it. Mrs. Durham was staring at us both as if we were common thieves.

"I got it, Grandma." Josh placed his hands on her shoulders.

"Joshua, these kids woke me from a sound sleep traipsing through our yard. And then I thought I heard some commotion way over here. What are they doing at my cottage?" She squeezed her eyes harder. "Is that you, Sam?" Her voice shook with anger.

"Grandma, I'm sorry. Please let me handle it."

Sam straightened up. "Mrs. Durham, I'm so sorry. I didn't realize this was your— "

"Sam, quiet," Josh ordered. "Grandma, it's my fault. I told them they could go swimming." He stepped in front of his grandmother to block her view. "I didn't think it would ever wake you up. I'm sorry it did. It was my fault. It won't happen again."

Mrs. Durham tried to shine her flashlight to get a closer look at me. "I don't care that they woke me up. I care that they're here. I told you this was off limits to your friends. Get them out."

Josh waited for her to get to the gate safely and turned his attention to us. He stood at the edge of the pool, arms flexed at his sides, silent.

"Oh, Josh. I'm so sorry." I tried to collect my breath as Sam floated too close to me. "It's not Sam's fault. He didn't know this was your grandma's place. We just got here a few minutes ago, really. I ... I wasn't thinking."

"Sorry, man." Sam smirked, eyebrows raised.

I pulled myself out of the pool and stood before him as the water rushed to the ground. "I'm so sorry. This is the first time I've ever brought anyone here, I promise."

Sam worked his way out of the pool and stood next to me with a sheepish grin swept across his face. "Dude, I really didn't mean to cause you trouble. But how is it that in all the years I've known you, I never knew this was your grandma's place? All those years we had to swim in that back pool with your grandma looking over at us— not getting away with anything. You've been holding out. I didn't know you had all this."

Josh blinked slow and shifted his jaw to the side. "It looks like you didn't know enough about either of us." He tilted his head in my direction. The words Sam said to me when Mrs. Durham interrupted turned in my mind. *I didn't know you were like this.*

I still worked to catch my breath. "I'm so sorry, Josh." He had risked his grandmother's opinion of him to give me a place to swim, and I had treated it like a playground with his own best friend.

Josh turned to Sam as if my words were irrelevant. "And you're here. With her?"

With her? Was it preposterous to Josh that Sam would actually spend time with me? *Like* me? Did he still think less of me because of the party those weeks ago?

We followed Josh on his silent march through the property. He was quiet and removed and didn't look back to let us know it would be all right. Sam's smirk had turned solemn. If he had been hoping to laugh this off, it was clear Josh wasn't going to let him. Worry etched across his eyes, and he returned to his SUV without another word. I had put him in this situation, and I didn't even warn him it was Josh's pool.

The fear sank in, the same fear that I had sensed in my mother when her men drove away after she had messed up, or got too drunk, or asked them for too much money. It was possible I had lost them both.

"Josh, I really am sorry. I didn't mean to take advantage. I just want you to know— "

He turned back to me, and my heart rose with expectation. "It's done," he said. "There's nothing else to discuss."

"Okay, good." I smiled, faking that I believed he was over it. But I could see something in his eyes. Was it disappointment? I couldn't live up to whoever he thought I was. "Josh, I don't want to lose you as a friend."

"We can't be friends, Melissa. Don't you see that?" He shut his eyes and shook his head free of some dark thought. "What are you doing with him? You are all wrong for him."

"All wrong for him? Why? You mean I'm not good enough for him."

I held my eyes on his face until he finally turned my way. I willed him to explain it. I wanted to hear him say it for himself: I wasn't good enough to be his girlfriend. I wasn't good enough to be Sam's either. I was the ugly duckling, with a wild mother and a brother who walked around dazed half the time. At best, I was his charity case.

"He comes from a different world, Missy."

"You think I don't know that?"

He shook his head. "That's not what I mean ..."

"And you're gonna help me instead, are you? Big brother? Like I'm so needy?"

Josh's eyes became slits. He forced quiet words through a clenched jaw. "Do you really think he understands you? Do you even think he wants to?" He opened his mouth but stopped himself and backed away. "I'm sorry. I can't talk about this. Good night."

Josh walked inside and left me standing between our houses alone, him going to his world and leaving me to mine. My eyes shut heavy that night. Sleep was easier than thinking of these things. I slept with my phone by my pillow waiting for a call from Sam, but nothing came. I awoke the next day at noon and left the key to the cottage on my windowsill. The cottage wasn't mine anymore.

• • • • •

"Come to the beach with me! It's warm enough now!" Crystal jumped on to the couch and buried her knees into my side. I groaned in pain. "I want to look for sand dollars!"

"No." I pulled her off the couch so I could see the TV. "I'm not in a good mood today."

"You promised."

I sighed and begged to go another day, but she was intent on the trip. She managed to drag Robby out of bed, and the three of us walked to the beach with his skim board in tow.

The Gulf reflected the perfect aqua blue of the sky and stretched before us against the powder white sand. On some days—when I needed it the most, it seemed—the island blushed with perfection like God's own personal postcard.

"Not even a ripple." Robby threw his board to the beach, dissatisfied.

I shoved him in the side. "It's gorgeous today, even if there are no waves." I dropped to a half whisper. "And this is Crystal's first real trip to the beach since we got back from Pennsylvania. She's too young to remember much from before we moved. It's a big day."

"Yeah, I guess you're right." He kicked the sand and inhaled dramatically. Suddenly, he roared like a lion, instantly transformed. "I guess that just means she has to go for it!" He scooped Crystal into his arms, and charged into the sea with a wild rush.

She squealed with excitement and clung to Robby's neck as he dunked under the surface and came back up again. He threw her into the air as high as he could make her go until she landed in the water, legs twisting in thrill and hysteria.

"Again! Again!" she shouted through laughter.

When Crystal finally collected herself, she begged us to help her find sand dollars. Robby and I smiled knowingly as she walked into the sand dunes to find them as if she was on a treasure hunt. Her eyes lit up with adventure when we explained she'd have to swim for them.

Crystal placed her hands on the skim board as we kicked into the Gulf, well over our heads until we reached the sandbar about a city block's length off shore. There we could stand. Even Crystal could keep her head above water as long as the tide stayed low.

“Now that we’re on the sandbar, you dig.” I raised my eyebrows to build the suspense. “They’re right under you.”

We plowed our toes through the sand until our feet were surrounded with a white cloud. Reaching down we pulled up shells and seaweed, and spit salt water on each other whenever we had a chance. And then we felt the flat, circular creatures under the pads of our feet. Crystal was in luck; we’d come across a bed of them. One by one we pulled them up, both small and large. Robby dove down to place a sand dollar between Crystal’s toes, and she shrieked at the thrill of finding one. He placed it on the palm of her hand and chuckled when she squealed as it sucked on her skin.

“They’re brown now, but they’ll turn white in the sun,” Robby explained.

We positioned the sand dollars on top of the skim board, and felt the gentle swell of the tide come in and the water get deeper. It was time to go in. After some deliberation, Crystal decided she would keep a select few and return the rest.

“I’m going to wait for these to get white in the sun. And then I’m going to break them,” she announced.

“Why would you do that?” Robby asked.

“The doves of peace are inside. And I want one for all of us to remember today.”

• • • • •

Josh and Sam sat on opposite sides of the lunchroom, passing each other with only vague nods as if words were too much effort. Their friendship seemed to dissolve overnight, and I had chosen my side by default because I was still holding his hand.

Sam retained his throne in the popular booths, and Josh faded into the poorly swept corners of the b-class tables. He looked remarkably comfortable there, as if he had been waiting to sit with the alternative kids for years and only now was set free to become something other than Sam's little buddy. It's remarkable how friendships can work for years, built on little more than Little League and study hall, until a trial comes and they disintegrate into ash. I couldn't imagine how it had all unraveled for good over the use of the cottage pool.

But I couldn't question it anymore, not when Sam seemed more determined than ever to make me his. He made that very clear when he pulled me to the side of his locker after class.

"I have something to ask you." His breath brushed my face.

"Ask away."

His eyes searched mine. "I know it's short notice, only a few weeks."

I stopped breathing to make sure I heard every one of his words.

"Would you like to go to prom with me?" He smiled bashfully. The question was so innocent and polite that it almost seemed like he didn't already know the answer.

"Prom?" I questioned in disbelief.

"Yeah, you've heard of it?"

I couldn't force the words past my throat. *Yes*, I nodded. *Yes.*

He smiled and lifted up my chin for a kiss. Mike and Ian heckled us from the other side of the hall.

"Okay, then," he said.

"Okay."

It was real. With one question from him, all my questions were settled. We were official. And he chose me. He. Chose. Me.

Chapter 10

Robby had been in the same pair of shorts for four days in a row. He delighted in resisting the masses at school, and our conservative, elderly neighbors, and even me. The more he skulked around the island in his cargo shorts and his ironic, 1970s T-shirts, the more girls who wore too many earrings and too much dark eyeliner seemed to flock to his side. It was an unusual logic bent on rebellion—teenage attraction.

Crystal didn't seem to mind the smell he slowly accumulated, a mixture of sweat and smoke and organic essential oils from his strange girls. She crawled onto his lap and mimicked his half-dazed lounge. There was something about the sight of her nestling her small platinum head under his chin that made me wonder if our tough surfer would rather be babysitting than hanging out with his raggedy friends. But even Crystal knew that duty would soon call, and Robby would be headed out to places that we would never be invited to.

"I can't stay here for long." Robby yawned and scratched the side of his cheek. "I have to go work on the boat today. I'm done with everything except the engine, and then I can take you out."

I sat down too close to him so he could be invaded by the sweet gooeyness of both his sisters. "How much longer?"

"Another few weeks of solid work, I think." Robby flipped the channels through Saturday morning cartoons until we settled on a Disneyesque sitcom whose two scenes alternated between a classroom and a soda shop.

Crystal's eyes flared at the sight of the characters flirting with each other in class. "I can't wait to be a big kid," she huffed.

Robby and I exchanged glances. If only our lives were like theirs. These TV kids spent high school learning lessons about why cheaters never win and how not to crash your parent's BMW. They weren't waiting on their mom's tips so they could buy a new pair of shoes. They weren't up at night looking through online phone listings to see if they could find their father's name. Robby looked at that show, assumed he'd never relate to the fair-haired kids on TV, and checked out. I looked at it and wondered what it would take to be just like them. I was closer now than I ever had been. I already had the best seat at lunch and a date to prom. One day soon maybe I would wake up and realize my life was finally perfect like theirs.

"You will be a big kid soon enough, Crystal," I said. "And you'll have a lot of fun."

Denise returned home from a morning visit to the beach with Bruce. From the neck down, her graceful, thin body was still damp with salt water. Her hair, however, hadn't seen a drop. My mother treated the water like an enemy to be reckoned with, a threat to her appearance. I don't know if anyone had ever pointed out to her that she lived on an island and was surrounded by it on all sides.

"We saw three dolphins today." Bruce entered the house with a towel hanging around his neck and sat at our kitchen table in wet shorts.

"Oh, yeah?" Robby sat up. "Black or gray?"

"Black porpoise. I haven't seen gray in a while, actually ..."

"Really?" Robby said. "I spot gray up by Longboat Pass all the time."

"Thatta boy, Robby." Bruce wiggled his brows. "It's good to keep an eye out for things like that cuz you'll need to know all this stuff when you work with the tourists. You help them find the dolphins and you'll be raking in the money."

Robby moved Crystal to his side and sat up straighter. There was a man in the house, and the fact deserved attention. There hadn't been a day in recent weeks when Bruce wasn't around. In the mornings he drank coffee with my mother, and in the evenings he waited to drive her home from work. On one occasion, he even fixed Crystal a bowl of cereal.

I began to associate the sound of her parking in the front with the husky rumble of his voice. They seemed to go from complete strangers to an old married couple in a matter of days.

And this, it seemed, is what happened with adults. There are only so many experiences a person can have until every new thing you try to do slips by default into the familiar groove you've been paving for years. The comfort of pouring two cups of morning coffee. The smell of a shower that's been used before you. The feeling of someone placing expectations upon you, that your life is no longer infinitely open but has limits, boundaries, a tether that makes you feel you belong. Whether Bruce and Denise really cared for each other or simply cared for the feeling of having each other, I will never know. It turned out a broken relationship was the feeling my mother was most comfortable with after all.

I had put off asking Denise for prom dress money for days, and it couldn't wait anymore. She had landed me a part-time job a few weeks earlier at the nearby grocery store because the manager liked her daiquiris. But the hours were sporadic and rare, and I had only managed to save half the money I needed. The only thing keeping me from trying to find my dress at Goodwill was how this conversation would go.

I trailed her into her bedroom and inhaled deeply. "Can I have some money for a prom dress?"

"For what?" As the question sank in she realized what I had said, but her face didn't budge. "Oh, Miss. I don't know about that. How much do you need?"

"Julie says they're at least one hundred dollars. I have about fifty."

"One hundred?" Her eyes bulged. "Where do you think you're going shopping, Park Avenue?"

"Mom, prom dresses aren't cheap anywhere. And maybe I won't spend all of it."

Denise nodded her head with a wry smile. "Right."

Bruce made his way to the doorway of her room and propped his arms on either side of the entryway, blocking us inside the cell with each other. "Prom sounds pretty important."

Denise locked her lips together as if he was right on cue.

"I'd like to help out, if you'd let me." He took a seat at the foot of my mother's bed, and I realized for the first time that I was the outsider in this room. Bruce was very much at home.

"You don't need to do that, Bruce." Denise smiled in my direction, the kind that told me she was going to have to fake a fight against him. "Missy has a job now, and I'm sure we can come up with the money. Sometime."

He waved his arms. "No, no. It's my pleasure, really. This is a special night and every girl needs to go to her prom in a nice dress."

Relief surged through my body, and I squealed with delight. My mother nodded her approval, and I hugged Bruce for the first time. He handed me a crisp one hundred dollar bill, and I was out of the house in a split second so he couldn't change his mind.

Julie knew how to make the most of every cent that came her way, which was a gift she possessed thanks to her shopaholic mother. We went to all the same stores we had gone to when she first shopped for her prom dress, which now were filled with girls from across Manatee County looking for last-minute solutions. Rayon and crinoline slipped over my head, one dress after the other.

The colors were bright and rich and a feast for my eyes: baby blue and emerald green and pink and black. Each gown squeezed over my hips and left a trail of sparkles around us on the dressing room floor. But Julie managed to unearth one with real potential. She rushed me in front of a mirror and held up a red satin gown.

"This is it." She held it to my face. "It doesn't have the neckline you wanted, but just trust me."

The crimson gown fell over my body with reckless confidence. I studied myself in the mirror, afraid to like it, as Julie held her breath.

"It's perfect." She sighed as she tugged at the sides and pulled the red material into place around my hips. "You won't even need to get it altered."

I exhaled with indecision. "Uh." No words formed in my head.

"Don't you like it?"

The dress conformed to my body like I was standing under a waterfall. It glided over my stomach and chest to make me look trim, and smooth, and full in all the places it mattered. I twisted as the light reflected different hues of red and ruby in its sheen. I looked older.

Julie leaned against the wall and hid her grin with her hand. "It doesn't matter what I think. Tell me what you're thinking."

"You picked a great dress."

"But?"

I looked at her in desperation. "I don't think I can pull this off."

She stepped toward me with a look of confusion. "What are you talking about?"

"It's too much." I grimaced at my reflection. "It's like something a model would wear. It's screaming 'look at me.'"

Julie placed her hands on my shoulders. "It's not too much. You are totally pulling it off. And you're beautiful in it."

Beautiful. Would Sam think so? My heart ached to hear it. I wanted to hear it again and again. But whenever I did, I assumed it was a lie. Something hollow inside knew that no matter how many times I heard the word, I would never really find my fill. I would never hear it enough to drown out the sound of Ian and his barking dogs. And this dress, staring back at me in its fiery brilliance, exposed me as false. Something so gorgeous, so hungry for attention, had no business on my body.

Julie squirmed in frustration. "Stop being so hard on yourself. Is that the only reason you don't like this dress? It's too pretty and might get you too much attention?"

I nodded.

"Then I overrule you. This is the one."

A few hours later she pulled up to my house, and I stepped out of the car with the gown on a hanger, covered in a plastic bag. I flattened my lips together in a tight line to keep from screaming from the excitement. It was all happening. I leaned through the passenger window. "Thank you. This is why you're my bestie—among other reasons, of course."

Julie sat up tall and laughed. "I know, right? Just enjoy this. It's prom!"

"Yeah. Hard to believe."

Her face straightened and she nodded in the direction behind me. "Looks like your neighbor's out."

I peeked to my side and saw Josh sitting in front of his garage, waxing his skim board.

"Is he still mad about the pool?" Julie rolled her eyes. I'd kept my promise and hadn't told Julie anything about the pool—until Sam and I got caught. Recently, I'd admitted everything. Well, at least everything I could admit out loud.

"I don't know. I gave up trying to figure him out, and I don't even really know if he's talking to me. He nods to me in the hallway. Does that count?"

"I guess." She twirled her hair. "Apparently he's taking Jenny Adams to prom."

I braced myself at the news. "Who's that?" I had never heard of her, not that it mattered to me. "I'm surprised he's even going. How do you know that, anyway?"

"Because JP's the biggest gossip on the island when he's not surfing. It's always the quiet ones. He knows everything that goes on out here. I guess she lives in Cortez Village, and Josh met her at church or something. I don't think it's serious, but whatever."

"Good." I stood up straight and slung the prom dress over my shoulder. "That's good for him."

She pulled away, and I turned around to face Josh as I returned to my house.

His forearm didn't stop working against his board, but his eyes were on me. "Hey."

"Hey." The pride left my chest the moment I saw him. I wanted to show him my dress and tell him that I was going to prom with Sam—that I wasn't from such a different world after all. But there was a distance in his eyes, and I reminded myself that he had never done anything unkind to me, except tell me I wasn't right for his one-time best friend.

• • • • •

It is an odd thing to be the unofficial girlfriend of the most popular junior in school. But it didn't sink in until I was back in science with Tanya Maldonado, who was whispering with her friends in the back of the room. And for the first time in as long as I could remember, I didn't have to worry if it was about me.

"Today, we're talking about the position of the Earth in our solar system." Ms. Bowie pushed her glasses toward her forehead as images of the Earth and sun flashed on the screen behind her. "Our galaxy, of course, is the Milky Way. This is just our little corner of the universe, our subdivision. And in the Milky Way alone there are billions upon billions of stars. Our star, of course, is the sun. If we were to compare the size of our solar system to the size of our galaxy, which houses it, it would be like our solar system was the size of a quarter compared to a galaxy that is the size of the entire North American continent. You may say, 'Ms. Bowie, that makes us feel small.' I don't mean to make you feel small. You *are* small. And we are just beginning to get to know how awesome our universe is."

Ms. Bowie assigned the class to work in small groups, which meant we had twenty minutes to gossip before shuffling together chicken scratch answers on a worksheet that no one cared about in the first place, because no one in the room was going to be excited about the Milky Way when our own universe was so much more meaningful.

Julie and I put our heads together and shared the latest details of our new romances.

"Look!" she exclaimed, her eyes on fire. She opened an intricately folded piece of notebook paper by pulling a tab that featured a rosebud drawn in number two pencil. Inside, the note read:

Julie, I can't stop thinking about you. –JP

I beamed in excitement for her. She was truly falling in love. I could see it in the way she sat up straighter at the sound of JP's name. It was too soon, I reasoned, for Sam to be sending such amazing notes. Our relationship was just beginning. But dating him had already saved me in a way I never thought would be possible. And this I discovered, ironically, from Tanya.

"Missy," she called in a whisper. "Hey, Missy."

Julie and I looked up from our blank worksheet to see Tanya waving us over to sit with her. "Hey, there's room over here."

I looked to Julie in momentary disbelief. We rose from our seats to join the semicircle of girls who had formed around Tanya.

"Yeah, we just thought we could get through this worksheet faster if we all worked on it together. By the way, that is totally the cutest dress you're wearing. I love it!" Tanya gushed.

"Oh, this?" I looked down at my outfit. "Thanks. It's Julie's, actually."

Tanya nodded with appreciation as Julie smiled self-consciously.

"Well, y'all have great taste." She raised her eyebrows in a perky show of appreciation. "So, does this class stink or what? I'm, like, help me stay awake already. When are we ever going to need to know the location of a certain star?"

"Seriously," I agreed. Tanya Maldonado was trying to be nice to me, and I was going to let her.

"So, Missy, what's new with you these days?" Shanice Hardy had blemish-free, mahogany-colored skin that seemed to look airbrushed even under the classroom's fluorescent lights. I knew little about her, except that she had made the varsity cheer squad long before anyone else in our grade, and she always seemed to be sitting right next to Tanya wherever Tanya was.

"Uh," I stalled. "Not much, I guess."

"Really?" she pressed. "Aren't you going to the prom with Sam King?"

Tanya smiled. "Don't bother her about that, Shanice. I mean, that's her business. Unless she wants to talk about it, that is."

All eyes were on me as they waited for a reaction. "Yeah, Sam's great," I confessed. The telltale blush shot across my cheeks as I realized I was the center of attention. "And prom should be great." *Everything's great. Don't I know another word?*

Tanya crossed her legs and leaned toward me. "Well, that's wonderful," she said. "I think it's cute. I mean, we all deserve somebody, right? Except for Ms. Bowie, that is."

Tanya watched our teacher walk the classroom in her ankle-length skirt and clunky brown shoes. Ms. Bowie was young, only a year or two out of college, but she dressed in baggy clothes that made her look twice her age.

"I mean, she's got to be so desperate. I'll bet you she's never been on a date. Don't you think?" Tanya looked to me for agreement.

I sat up in my desk. "Oh. Yeah, totally." The guilt panged me in the side at once. Ms. Bowie had never been anything but nice to me, and I hadn't been in the cool-girl circle more than five minutes before I was picking the supposedly lesser beings apart. But the only thing scarier to me than becoming one of the mean girls was becoming my old self again.

When Ms. Bowie called Julie and me back to our seats, I felt the long gaze of the rest of the class follow me across the room. Something about the world as we had all understood it had just changed.

• • • • •

Sam didn't bring up the plan for the post-party until prom was one week away. We'd go to Ian's riverfront house, where the boys had never planned for anything in more painstaking detail.

Parents out of state. Rooms empty. Father's liquor cabinet stocked three rows deep.

This was not the usual post-prom party as I understood it. It was going to be, by careful design, a small group of couples who had arranged confirmed alibis to be at parent-chaperoned events, but who would, indeed, be pulling secret stashes of overnight clothes from their car trunks and keeping a tight watch on the neighbors to make sure they didn't get busted. Ian's house, it was rumored, boasted a waterfall over the pool, two spare refrigerators stocked with extra food, and a speakerphone on the gate. If Sam and I came from two different worlds, I should need a passport to enter Ian's.

But it was Denise, and not prom night, that preoccupied my thoughts prior to the dance. On Sunday morning of the week leading up to the big day, I awoke to the sound of another man in our kitchen. Robby had been out all night, and so he wasn't there to share my initial shock when Hawaiian Shirt Ray asked my mother where she kept the coffee creamer. Nothing made sense — I had last seen him racing away on his motorcycle.

I could tell from the way Denise refused to make eye contact with me that he had not just arrived that morning.

"Hey, kiddo," he called to me as I made my way to the living room and practically fell onto the couch.

I wondered if he knew my name. I didn't respond.

Crystal rested her head on my lap as if to feign fatigue. Even at seven, I knew she could see the storm brewing.

Denise nervously prepared breakfast. She set a bowl of cereal in front of Crystal's chair without a word and towered over Ray as he drank his coffee too slowly. "I'm so sorry to say this, but I have a lot to do today before I head in to work."

Ray sipped the coffee unaware the comment was an implied order to get out of her house. "Well." I didn't like the look that crept into his eyes then. "You shouldn't stay out so late at night."

He reached behind her to stroke the back of her knee, and she backed up instinctively. I could see the scene clearly in my mind. My mother took the late shift at the restaurant, stayed afterward for a nightcap with the bartender, ignored the good advice of her manager to go home, and Ray settled in to rekindle an old flame. I wondered how long Bruce had been out of sight that day until the unquenchable loneliness that always undermined my mother's relationships set in. Had Bruce spoken an unkind word or cheated on her? Probably not. But had he made the mistake of departing the restaurant at a respectable hour, leaving her open to Ray's advances? Had he turned out not to have as much money as he ought to for a man who watched over the sailboats of German tourists? Germans always paid for the best, after all. Bruce had probably turned his back for not even a moment by the time Denise had counted all the reasons he was denying her of something she needed. And with that, she swiveled on her barstool to flash her infectious smile at Ray because he was handy, and spent the rest of the night feeling entirely justified.

The next morning was always a different story. She rubbed the kitchen counter in tiny circles where there were no stains. "Sorry, Ray. I just have a lot to do with the kids today."

I rolled my eyes at her lie.

And then, as if on cue, Bruce wandered through the door with a box of doughnuts to surprise us. As he stepped into the living room, Crystal's eyes lit up in excitement. He stopped himself before he reached the kitchen. Oddly, he didn't even look surprised. Just disappointed.

"Bruce!" Denise stepped between the men as if she could hide them from each other. "What a surprise, baby! You brought doughnuts for the girls?"

Ray stood up from his chair with mouth tightly shut, waiting for Bruce to make the next move.

"You have a guest?" Bruce eyed Ray with disgust.

"Uh, yeah. This is Ray. You may know him from the restaurant. He just stopped by to say hello."

Ray didn't cover for her. Not that I blamed him — she had actually managed to do this to him *twice*. He mumbled a curse, stomped past Denise, and brushed Bruce's shoulder as he slammed the front door behind him.

And then the begging began.

Crystal and I retreated to my room. I knew how it would play out. She would bang on his chest and deny everything he had just seen. In another three minutes she'd admit it all. She'd throw her arms around him and promise that her infidelity was only due to stress or work or concerns over us kids. She would never do it again.

But I knew Bruce well enough to know that he would never give her the chance. Crystal and I put on our swimsuits, and I snuck her out my bedroom window. We ran to the beach.

The water offered a sharp contrast to the storm unfolding inside our house. It was flat and turquoise, and I wondered if I could swim across it for hours before hitting the first disruptive ripple. I would do anything to escape the island.

• • • • •

We didn't see Robby that day, or the next, and I wondered if he had found out about my mother's break from Bruce. His room gave evidence that he had stopped by the house for a moment, ransacked his dirty laundry for more T-shirts, and slipped out the door before we noticed he was there. Tuesday after school, Denise began to question me.

"And just where the heck is your brother these days? He comes in and out of here like this is a motel."

"I don't know."

"Well, have you seen him at school?"

"Not today."

"I'm getting pretty sick of this, and I'm starting to worry. See if you can go find him. Maybe he's down there working on that boat." Denise's bottom lip trembled just a bit, and I could tell she was sincere.

I rode my bike to the docks and was just approaching the parking lot when shouts radiated from the marina shop. As I walked toward the building, Robby stormed out, throwing the door shut behind him. Before I could stop him, he jumped into his friend's car. They peeled out of the lot, music blasting from the windows.

The smell of rotting fish and day-old beer reached me before I got inside. Behind a counter, Bruce was plotting a course on a nautical map. A cigarette hung from his mouth and smoke wrapped around him in a thick haze that warned me to get away.

"Was that my brother who was just in here?" I wanted to hear him admit it.

He didn't look up from the map until I stood in front of him for another ten seconds, and when he spoke it was tinged with disdain. "So? What do you want from me?"

"Were you fighting with each other?"

"What's it to you?" He folded the map and busied himself behind the counter with a logbook.

"I haven't seen him in a day or two, and I'm wondering what's going on."

"Well, that's funny, because I haven't been able to get rid of him. You mind your own business and get away from that crazy family of yours the first chance you get. That's what you ought to be doin'. Not lookin' for that punk."

"Punk? Isn't he working for you?" I placed both hands on his counter and made it clear I wasn't going to leave until he answered.

"No. That's history." Bruce finally looked up to meet my eyes, softening just enough to give me the answer I needed. "He came back again today to beg for his job back. But I'm not interested."

"I don't understand. He's been working on that boat with everything he has for you. I don't get it."

"It's over."

"But he's been working for free for a couple of months now. You had a deal."

Bruce blew smoke inches from my face. All kindness was gone. "It was a favor, not a deal. And I don't want any of that woman's brood around here."

"You fired him because of my mother?"

"I told you, it's none of your business. Get outta here."

"Anything about my brother is my business." Anger spiked through my body.

Bruce shook his head and pounded a fist on the counter. "Fine. I'll tell you what I told him. The truth is your mother is a good-for-nothin' tart. She's been with half this island and she lies through her teeth. I shoulda never had anything to do with her or her lousy son.

You try and do somebody a favor and this is what you get. I don't want to see her or anybody who knows her within one hundred feet of my property. That's what I told your brother, and that's what I'm telling anybody who will listen. Now leave."

I tried to collect my breath, but the pain in my stomach would hardly allow me to stand. I felt like I had just been punched in the gut. I knew that Bruce was finished with my mother, but I hoped, at least, he'd still honor his promise to my brother. I didn't think an adult would break a promise to a kid. Not like that.

He rounded the corner and hovered over me. "You got your little prom dress. That's all you're getting out of me. Do yourself a favor, sweetie, and leave that house before you turn out just like them."

The vein bulged on the side of his head, and sweat seeped from his chest and into the old T-shirt stained with fish guts and grease. My knees felt like they were missing bone, and my bottom lip began to shake. I was lucky to still be standing.

"But I don't understand. Robby didn't do anything to you." I blinked back tears. I knew what this boat had meant to my brother, and I knew he had been working with Bruce long before Denise began her fling.

"That boat wasn't going anywhere, anyway. Your brother didn't know what he was doing." Bruce turned and left for the back office.

I summoned the strength to leave the shop and left the brooding, angry giant inside.

My mother had not only lost her man and what modicum of a reputation she had maintained on the island. She had lost my brother's job for him, one of the only good things I had seen Robby do since we moved back.

I returned home and stretched out on my bed in silence. Denise had gone to work. Crystal put herself to bed. And I did not move for three hours.

Late that evening, Robby returned as the neighborhood grew

silent with the early moments of sleep. He still wore his faded cargo shorts.

I stood in his bedroom doorway. "I know what happened, Robby. I went down to the marina to look for you."

"No big deal." He grunted and tossed a few shirts from a pile on the floor. Dirty clothes were thrust into his backpack and the penny jar emptied of its coins.

"Where are you going?" I sat on his bed watching him rip through his room in a frenzy.

"Nowhere."

"Robby?" I pressed.

"I need to get out of here. I don't know what I'm going to do if I see her. I just have to get away for a little while. A friend told me I could crash at his place, so I'll be there a couple days. Just tell Mom I'm okay. I can't handle her drama."

"Which friend? Not Ricky Brewer?"

"I've been staying with Ricky a lot. But, no. Tonight I'm staying next door."

My breath caught. "Josh?"

"Yeah," Robby said. "Mom probably won't even notice I'm gone."

"She's noticed."

"Yeah, well. It doesn't change anything."

Tears began to well in his eyes but he choked them back. "I knew the second I saw him that I couldn't really trust him, not really," Robby said. "Though Mom must have screwed him over good. I went from being his long-lost son to a trespasser in the span of two days. Do you know he threatened to call the cops on me if I came back to work on that boat again? He didn't even look me in the eye when he said it. I wasn't even worth talking to."

I placed my hand on his shoulder until he moved it away with a jerk.

"I worked on that piece of crap boat for two months for free, and now he's just going to take it and run?" The anger came back and the tears rushed to escape his eyes. He wiped them away harshly. "Why do I even bother trying? It always comes to this. It always comes to something totally messed up. It's like we're nobodies, and we never had a chance at being anything but nobodies. Why are we even here?"

"Don't say that, Robby," I cried. "Mom did this. Not you. She messed up. Not you. And Bruce is a jerk. Anybody else would have kept his promise to you because you were doing such good work."

"Yeah. Well I guess if that was true, the boat would be working right now, wouldn't it?"

He threw the backpack over his shoulder and walked next door. I saw Mrs. Durham's lights turn on, and I watched through my window as Robby hid his bike on the other side of Josh's house.

When Denise got home from the late shift, I admitted to her that Robby was staying next door. She didn't go to see him, like I thought she would. She nodded quietly and went to her room. The door shut behind her. It was the loneliest I had ever seen her.

Chapter 11

I'm going to have the most beautiful prom date ever." Sam lifted up my chin and winked. "So you can't be sad. Sad's not pretty."

I nodded. "I know. I'm fine. Nothing's wrong." We only had a few seconds alone at the booths until the rest of his gang arrived and our privacy was destroyed. He was right even if he didn't know what was going on at home. I needed to be happy, or at least look it. I needed to give Robby some space and let him come back when he wanted.

The seats filled with Sam's friends. They were my friends too now, I supposed. I knew the names of their siblings and what their parents did for a living. These characters who once played the simple roles in my life — observers and villains — now occupied my world in 3D. And they were proving themselves to be human, however unaware they were of their effect on those who sat on the other side of the cafeteria. I was increasingly unaware as well. All of that seemed to fade into the distance when there was so much else going on.

"I need to get something to drink. I'll be right back."

When I walked over to the beverage area, I saw Josh digging through some cartons to pull out a container of whole milk. I snuck up behind and peered over his shoulder.

"You're the only person in the whole school who drinks whole milk other than the offensive line," I said. It was the first full sentenced I had managed to speak to him since the pool.

He turned to me with soft eyes and no smile. I stepped back. I wanted to hate him, even if I knew it was an unjustified sort of hate. He was meddling in my life again. He knew all my secrets once more. He knew how far my reality was from what I wanted Sam King to see. He knew that Sam had no idea my mother was an island joke and my brother was a stoner runaway. Josh's theory about my world being so different from Sam's, from the good world, was so true it was taking up space in his spare bedroom. But he had given my brother a place to stay, and this trumped my annoyance at the times he had tried to keep me from enjoying Sam's attention.

"Thanks for taking my brother in. That's all I wanted to say."

"Of course." Josh walked toward me until I backed up against the lunchroom wall. "You told your mom, I'm guessing?"

"Yeah." I hated how nervous I felt around him. "If I didn't she'd just freak out. At least she knows he's all right."

"I don't see much of him, you know. He comes and goes as he pleases."

"I saw him in the hall this week, so I guess he's back in class?" I asked.

Josh shrugged.

"So, how does he seem?"

"Lost."

It was precisely the right word. "And over a stupid boat. I mean, why was that boat so dang important to him anyway? It's not like he can't go out and get another one if he saves up. And if he stopped hanging out with those potheads, he'd have more going for him. He aggravates me so much sometimes."

"Bruce was taking him under his wing and just cast him out. Pretty big rejection."

The words cut through my gut until anger at Denise welled up to fill the hole inside me. I wanted to scream at her, and I wanted that moment back in the shop with Bruce so I could tell him what I thought of him too. "I want to shake him and force all of this mess out of his head."

"Yeah, and get him to fit in and sit at the popular booths like you?" Josh said with a bite. "Then it would all be straightened out?"

I shook my head and stepped away. There he was again, reminding me that I didn't belong and that my brother didn't belong. "Whatever."

"We're talking," Josh called out to me as if to make up for his offense. "Robby and I are talking about stuff, and I'm sure he'll be back home soon. My grandma loves him. I think she loves him more than me ..."

I forced a small smile. It felt like he was trying to give me something hopeful, even if it wasn't everything I wanted to hear. "Thanks. And thanks for talking to me again."

"I never stopped," Josh said.

When I made it back to the booths, Sam wrapped his arm around me and shot a smirk to Josh across the cafeteria. "Was that Josh you were talking to for so long?"

"Yeah."

"What were you talking about? Was he inviting us to another pool party?" Sam looked at me mischievously and tapped my nose with his finger.

"That's not funny. Let's not even bring that up."

Sam planted a long kiss on me and everyone at the booths oohed at the PDA in full, undeniable display. Streaks of red crossed my cheeks when we were finished. He wasn't ashamed of me. He didn't think we were from two different worlds. And if he did, he didn't care.

That evening, Crystal had figured out that Robby was staying next door and had made her way into the Durham house looking for our brother. Josh's grandmother sent her back with a plateful of homemade cookies and a story about Michigan winters.

"Did you know there's still snow on the ground up north right now?" Crystal stuffed chocolate goo into her mouth until crumbs burst from the sides. "Robby says he's coming home tonight. But I wouldn't want to leave either if I could eat all these cookies."

Moments later Robby snuck into my room with an impish grin and threw a paper plane to the foot of my bed. It was another one of his drawings, a portrait of me wearing a tiara and a prom dress. It was signed with his signature water symbol and initials.

"Welcome back, stranger," I said.

"Yeah."

"Mom'll be glad."

"So, prom tomorrow?" he asked, changing the subject.

"Yep."

"I'm going too." He stood up tall and smoothed down his hair for effect.

I rushed up from my bed and pointed into his chest. "Who are you taking?"

"Lisa from up the street. No big deal. Just friends."

"Mmm-hmm," I teased. And then I saw a redness in his eyes. As I looked closer, he looked away. "What's up with your eyes? You look like a vampire or something. Are you high?"

"Step back, little sister." I guess I would never know. He waved me away as if my question was ridiculous. He backed against the wall and laughed. "I'm cool. And I'm wearing a kilt to prom cuz, well, why not?"

"They'll kick you out just like they did that senior. He was suspended for wearing it to homeroom."

"It's prom. Let them try." Robby went to his room and shut the door, and I was glad to have my brother back in whatever condition he managed to return.

On Saturday, my mother cooked us a full breakfast, and no one brought up Bruce or the boat or my brother's week abroad. Julie burst through our front door with a bag full of makeup and hair tools. "This is an all-day primping session, and you're not even off the couch yet!"

I pulled an old afghan over my head and swatted her away. "It's too early!"

"It's eleven o'clock already! Besides, it's never too early to get ready for prom."

Denise laughed. "Julie is right about these things. It's best not to fight her, honey."

Crystal jumped on to my back and needled her knee into my side. "Get up! Get up! Get up!" she sang. "It's time to look beautiful!"

"Ouch!" I stretched begrudgingly. "Okay! Okay! I'm up!"

I was ready to wear my red satin dress. I was going to take Sam's breath away. The rest of the day went something like this:

Paint toes. Spill polish on carpet. Clean up with polish remover. Cover stain with old towel.

French manicure. Ruin pinky finger. Redo pinky finger.

Diet coke. Carrot sticks.

Shower.

Shave. Knick knee. Shave around knick in careful ninja razor move.

Give Robby exactly ten minutes of bathroom time before resuming command.

Blow dry. Twist. Pin.

Brush out.

Twist again. Pin again.

Spray. Spray. Spray.

Repeat for Julie.

Spray.

Pin bejeweled barrette in Julie's hair.

Require Robby to ooh and ahh at hair feat.

Split a sandwich.

Lotion everywhere.

Begin fragrance layering.

Makeup.

Eyeliner disaster. Baby oil on Q-Tip.

Smoky eyes!

Julie returns home.

Sit perfectly still for one hour and thirty minutes until Sam arrives.

Crystal kept watch the entire time with her nose pressed to the living room window. When Sam finally arrived in his father's sedan, she screamed with delight and ran around in hyper little circles. "He's here! He's really here!"

"Calm, little one. You have to calm down!" I ordered. "Remember, we're totally cool and relaxed."

Crystal opened the door to let him in, his dimples leading the way. Sam wore a black tuxedo with a scarlet cummerbund that complemented my dress perfectly. He looked like he had just stepped off the red carpet, drastically out of place next to the torn couches and stained lampshades inside our humble rented home. It was the first time he had been inside.

"You look really good." He looked me up and down without apology.

"Thanks."

"Like really hot." He puckered his lip and raised his eyebrows as if to show his appreciation.

Crystal started to giggle until I ordered her across the street to her babysitter.

"Wait! I have something for you!" She ran to her room and retrieved a white shell.

She handed me the small, frail object. It was in the shape of a white dove.

"This is from the sand dollars we took out of the beach, isn't it?"

She nodded with a wide smile. "I have one for Robby, and one for you, and one for me. And I have more. That was fun. Remember?"

"I remember."

She finally ran across the street, and I stuffed the white shell in my borrowed purse that matched my borrowed shoes. Sam leaned in to kiss me. When he pulled back, his lips were smudged with red lipstick.

"My mom wants us to drive down to the restaurant where she works. Would that be okay? She just wanted to see me and meet you."

"Anything you want."

When we arrived at the grill, Denise was serving a table on the deck. She looked up from her customers and gushed at the sight of us. "You kids look gorgeous!"

She crossed the maze of tables in a flurry of gushes until all eyes were on us. "And it's so nice to meet you, Samuel. Missy's told me so much about you. I understand you play football and that you live in town. And you're a very good student too, I presume. And tall! Oh, I like the tall ones. Oh, Missy, this one's a keeper, I can tell!"

If I tried to bite my nails at this point it would have ruined my manicure, and so there was no relief from the embarrassment I was suffering. I stood on the deck of a public restaurant as complete strangers heard every thought that crossed my mother's mind about the most important date I had ever been on. But something about me didn't mind. I was ready to be seen. Sam made polite remarks and then nudged me in the side to say it was time to leave.

Denise made a tourist take our picture, and we were finally off to dinner with most of the people who sat with us every day at the booths. This time, though, we placed our napkins in our laps and chuckled as we tried to discern which fork to use for our salads.

Sam had never been this attentive before. Once we were at prom, if I needed a drink, he was pouring it. When I asked to sit down, he stayed by my side. When I watched Tanya Maldonado arrive with the senior class president, a boy who was likely her fallback date, Sam told me that he thought I was the prettiest girl in the room. It was as if he had read every Jane Austen romance in the past week, and he was putting it into full practice that night. And the best part, the best part of all, was that he never stopped touching me. If we stood, he touched his hand to mine. If we danced, he held my waist. If we walked to the other side of the room, his hand was on the small of my back. He was an escort. A true gentleman. And I felt like nobility. For the first time in my life, I felt the sheer power of what it was like to be envied by all the other girls around me.

"You're the perfect date," I sighed.

He leaned in for a kiss, his blue eyes sparkling beneath the disco ball. I smiled. I loved the feeling of being able to turn his head and command his attention. As his lips approached mine, I did a double take at the sight behind him. It was Josh and Robby with their dates. Robby stood aloof as his date Lisa stared at him for attention. His kilt hung boldly over his legs, as if he was daring a teacher to create a scene. Josh nodded his head to the music as his date fidgeted with her dress. I wondered if she was the girl from Cortez that I had heard about—the mysterious girl who Josh actually thought was good enough for him.

"Your brother's in a skirt," Sam announced.

"It's a kilt."

"That's supposed to be some kind of statement?"

"Oh, who knows," I said. "Let's just dance, okay?"

I wanted to feel the safeness of Sam's shoulder against my cheek, and I didn't want to look for another minute at my shocking brother or my neighbor who knew me better than he should. Tonight, I was a princess.

We danced in the center of his friends. Sam spun me out and pulled me in close. He dipped me slowly as I tried not to laugh. This was what I had dreamed of since I was thirteen. Sam thought I was gorgeous.

"Let's get out of here," he said. "Ian just gave me a nod, and I think they're all ready to head back to his place now. Sound good?"

"Sounds perfect. Just give me a second."

I crossed the dance floor to say hello to my brother for the first time that night. His friends were gathered around him in hysterics as he danced wildly in his kilt, his feet flailing like a puppet. He was doing something between an Irish jig and the running man.

I tapped on his shoulder to interrupt the routine. "Hey."

He turned around abruptly and his eyes landed on me with a smile. "Sis!"

"Nice moves. I was just coming by to tell you I'm outta here."

"Where you going?"

I tilted my head in annoyance. "Nowhere."

"Ian Owen's house?"

"How did you know that?"

Robby gestured to his side, where Josh was leaning against the ballroom wall.

Our neighbor looked to be suffocating in his tuxedo, the bow tie loosened around his neck. Spotlights danced across his face and reflected off of his eyes like glass. He looked at me and shifted his jaw just a bit to the side. It was half of a smile. And the other half of his face was intent. Earnest. He didn't look like a guy at a dance. He looked like a man intent on guarding someone, but his date was nowhere to be seen. There was only Robby. And now me.

Robby wiped his upper lip from sweat and stepped in closer. "Why don't you hang out with me tonight instead? It'll be fun. We're going out to Coquina."

"The beach? No, I don't think so."

"Come on," he sang. He surely knew it was a futile effort.

"No, I have to stay with Sam. My date? We're going to Ian's house."

Robby nodded in resignation. "Fine."

"Fine," I repeated. I softened my tone. "I'm glad you came. I didn't think you would. Try not to get picked up by the cops tonight."

He raised his finger and pointed at me like a father giving a lecture. "All right, Melissa Anne Keiser. Don't you worry about me. *You* be good."

I rolled my eyes. "Okay. Well, see ya."

He reached for my arm but missed it by a few inches. His hand went limp. "Hey, I love you, sis."

I smiled. "I love you too, Robby."

As I turned away, I caught an empty look in his eyes. It was a faraway sort of stare that was filled with neither disappointment nor hope—just a haunting, vacant gaze that seemed not to focus on anything in its path. It was as if he was seeing something that I couldn't, and he had been looking at it so long that he was simply left numb. If it had been any other day or any other moment, I would have gone back to ask him if he was fine. I would have pressed the truth out of him, because a look like that had no place at a prom when he was dancing in a kilt next to his friends. But Sam was already pulling me away. And so I turned my back and followed my date out of the ballroom.

• • • • •

Ian's mansion of a house was starting to settle into dim lights and whispers, until the only thing that managed to keep my attention was Sam's hand around my waist.

He leaned in and pressed his forehead to mine. "Let's go tour the house."

I swallowed to stall. I knew exactly what that meant. They practically taught that line in health class.

Sam waited patiently for my response until I finally convinced myself I could handle whatever the tour would bring. I nodded my permission, and he grinned widely as he took my hand.

"No way!" Ian yelled. His face was pressed against the living room window. "I thought everyone knew this party wasn't going to be big."

Sam exhaled in frustration and rushed to Ian's side to look through the window. He broke into laughter. "Dude. Guess plans have changed."

"No way. No way. *No way!*" Ian marched around his living room in circles as he talked to himself. "I'll just stand by the door and tell all of them the situation."

The situation was two dozen cars packed with prom goers moving up Ian's driveway. And there were more on the street, all lined up to park on his father's front lawn. All with anxious dates inside who were looking for a place to land. And each would surely know Ian and claim to be his friend.

Ian opened the front door and waved his arms. "Hey, guys. Sorry, but you can't party here."

Mike Lewis walked up with his date on his arm.

"Hey, Mike. Well, you're okay, but no one else," Ian stammered.

Then came Tanya Maldonado and Shanice Hardy, with four other girls tethered to their sides with dates in tow.

Ian nodded. "Tanya, Shanice. How are my girls? Well, you guys can come in, but I really can't have a big party here. Everyone else is gonna have to go."

Sam and I took a seat on the couch, and he shook his head. "Just sit back and watch, Missy."

They poured in through the door like someone had released a teenage dam. It happened so quickly that I stopped counting after the seventy-first person plodded through Ian's door, over his mother's oriental rug, into the Italian marble kitchen, and up the stairs to wherever Sam had been hoping to give me a tour.

Ian rubbed his forehead and took a seat next to me. "This wasn't the plan."

I tried not to laugh.

"And if I call the cops, they're going to call my parents, and my parents are gonna come home early. And then it'll just be worse."

Sam nodded in agreement. "That's about it."

Ian tapped his foot as kids raided his father's liquor cabinet. "I need to control this as much as I can so the cops won't come. I need some enforcers."

Sam pursed his lips together. "No way, man. No way."

Ian slapped him on the shoulder. "I wouldn't ask if I didn't need this."

"Ugh, this sucks." Sam sighed. He turned to me and explained. "Ian wants me to get my big brothers. They used to be club bouncers back in the day. Everybody's still afraid of them."

Ian practically jumped up and down in his seat. "Yeah, yeah. That's all we need, and we can keep this thing under control. Come on, Sam. I wouldn't ask if I didn't need them."

Sam tucked his finger under my chin and kissed me on the cheek. "I'll be right back. They won't come if I just call them."

I sunk into the couch and watched Ian's house boil over with half our high school. My date had abandoned me. JP and Julie, who'd snagged original invites, were nowhere to be found; no doubt doing something romantic like I should be doing.

Minutes passed. Then hours. No one had heard from Sam. He didn't answer his phone. Finally, the roar of the party died into tired lulls of sleepy laughter. Kids passed out on the couches, and under the dining room table, and wherever they could find a place to rest. The smell of old popcorn and pizza filled the air. And even when the party was definitely over, Sam hadn't returned.

I leaned my head back against the sofa cushion and surrendered my eyelids to the weight of sleep. I had to assume Sam was okay, that he could take care of himself. When I awoke, a pair of familiar blue eyes was staring at me, but they were foreign at the same time. My shoulders were shaking from someone's hands pressing on me to wake me up.

"Missy? Are you Missy?"

I stirred with a shudder. "Yes."

The boy looked like Sam, but he wasn't Sam. And he wasn't a boy. He was older, close to a man. "I'm Sam's brother. You have to come with me."

I could see dread in his eyes, apprehension that refused to tell me anything else.

"Where?"

"I need to take you home. That's all I know. Will you come with me?"

Chills popped across the back of my head and down my arm. Something wasn't right, and no one was awake to explain it. I gathered my purse and followed the tall, strange man out of the house and into his pickup truck. We drove back to the island as sunlight began to crest behind us. I knew better than to ask any questions. A part of me didn't want to hear whatever answers he had. But I knew who he was, and that he knew what was going on.

Chapter 12

Two police cruisers were parked along the ditches of my street, lights off, empty. Neighbors stood at the edge of their driveways—arms crossed against their chests, eyes following us as Sam's brother pulled into my driveway. He cut the engine but stayed in the truck as I headed into my house.

All I could think was, Why are we at my house?

Through the front screen door I could see my mother smoking, shaking, sitting with two officers on our living room couches. I straightened out my red dress and opened the door in silence.

"Where were you?" Denise turned to me with accusation in her eyes. Mascara smudged the side of her cheek, and her voice was hoarse. "I called for you at Julie's and you weren't there."

I turned to an officer. "What is going on in here?"

My mother gasped for air as muddled cries escaped her throat. Josh surfaced from the kitchen.

"What are you doing here?" I asked him.

"I haven't been here long. We just got back from the hospital." He stepped toward me, hands gently stretched out. Sam trailed behind him.

"Mom, why won't anyone say what's going on? What is it?" My legs froze to their place in the middle of the living room. I couldn't bring myself to walk any farther.

"Robby," she cried. "Robby. My baby, Robby. I ... I can't say it." She shook her head and looked to one of the officers.

A short man in uniform wrung his hands. "I'm sorry, honey. I have very bad news."

I remember the feel of the carpet underneath my knees, and I remember Josh catching my fall. There was a party, and there were drugs. And the people there said he was taking them all night. They found him in his friend's car when they started to leave, with a note on the dash that read, "I'm sorry." The hospital would have to confirm, but it looked like an overdose of everything he could get his hands on. And no one seemed to know he had too much. No one noticed when he headed out of the house and into a parked car to go to sleep. Two of his friends admitted he'd said he wished he could get away for good, but neither of those two thought much of it until they went out to the car to wake him up. And, no, I wasn't allowed to see him now. Robby was dead.

I screamed but no sound came out. My throat cracked, and I forgot to breathe. "Why can't I see him? I want to see him *right now*!"

I pushed Josh and Sam away from my side and stumbled to Robby's bedroom.

Crystal was there, singing to herself as if she couldn't hear us in the living room, turning his paper airplanes in her hand. She lay at the foot of his bed. Her platinum hair stretched over his rumpled sheets. Robby would have smiled if he found her like that, so innocent and sweet.

But my brother was never coming home.

• • • • •

This is how it is when someone you love dies, when someone you truly love leaves you. The first feeling isn't grief. It's shock. I stood still, but the rest of the world didn't.

The house filled with people in the days that followed. They cut paths in the hallway carpet, fixing us coffee, asking us questions, moving. They slept and woke. They ate meals, and they placed glasses of ice water on my bedside table.

It couldn't be undone. I couldn't get that night back. And I couldn't go back to the four hundred moments when someone could have stopped this, when I could have stopped this. Everyone around me was in the present, and I was searching for a way to get to the past. If I could just see him. If I could just smooth back his shaggy hair, I knew his eyes would open again and he would be all right.

I didn't leave my room for longer than a few hours until the day of the funeral. Mrs. Durham laid a dress on my bed. Their church would hold the service, and their cemetery would hold his grave.

Crystal's father arrived and extended his arm to my mother as she walked down the long church aisle dressed in black. He rubbed Crystal's back when she asked if Robby was in the coffin. It was the first time I had heard his name in seventy-two hours, and it stung my heart on impact.

A woman I had never seen before hung my brother's class photo on an easel and looked at me as if she understood. And every kid—every kid from our high school, it seemed—filled the pews until a crowd collected at the back and crept up the sides. They had come to honor my brother, or because they suddenly felt a connection to him now that he was gone, or because everyone else was going to the service. I didn't begrudge them their grief. I was pleased to see that there was a room full of people who might not ever forget him. And if we all lived on for seventy more years, the earth would be forced to remember him for at least that long.

Sam pulled his arm around me dutifully. When he had left Ian's house that night to drag his reluctant brothers from their apartment, Josh called him from the hospital, where he was holding my mother's hand. Sam couldn't bear to tell me, and he couldn't lie if he went to collect me at Ian's house. He sent his brother to retrieve me and waited for me until we pulled into the driveway, trembling because he didn't have the words.

As he sat in the pew at my side, his foot tapped in a nervous insect kind of way as if he had stumbled into an exam he knew he couldn't pass. And I was grateful for his tapping foot. It was a far better thing to focus on. It would have been better if I could have just fallen asleep right there and tucked myself into the shadowed dip of Sam's neck to forget what my eyes had seen. My sister, working to make sense of my brother's coffin. My mother's relatives, who hadn't called on us in years, weeping. The somber, earnest, anguished face of Josh, his eyes fixed on me, his suntanned cheeks looking vulgar inside the pale church—browned as if to flaunt the fact that the sun was still shining outside.

I resented everyone in the church for having a heartbeat, I resented the eighteen-year-old boy in the wooden box, and I questioned who would have given him so much power so young in life that he could ruin everything. How could any one person make a decision that is so permanent, that could never be undone? How could my brother be dancing and then end his life four hours later? Had we all missed the signs? How lost Robby was?

I hated the organ that was playing and the scent of the lilies and the dank, ancient smell of the wooden walls made soft from the wet Florida air.

The pastor cleared his throat and stepped down from the podium, where someone had positioned a microphone. He walked into the aisle and stood two feet from me. The first words he spoke were about God as our refuge and strength, that he was present in our times of trouble. That God loved Robby.

Did God love my brother? If so, where was God when Robby needed him? Where is God now?

"We should ask questions during this difficult time," the pastor went on. "We should not stop until we find their answers, even if they seem like they're too much to bear. Because no matter what the answers are, they will lead us back to the greater truth. They will lead us back to God's goodness to redeem, and back to loving each other — more and more."

I stared at my lap. All of this was easy for him to say. He'd never lived in a family where love was something you had to grasp for, something that could leave you in a moment. Had never lived with the question of whether he could have loved his brother a little more.

"The truth is the Lord loves each of you more than you can comprehend, and he will move heaven and earth to bring you close to him. God is good, and because of that there is hope we will get to see Robby again one day, in a place where the Most High dwells, where the light of his goodness is so bright we will no longer have any need for the sun.

"We cannot know what goes on between a man and God. So hope with me that Jesus has restored Robert, in his great love, to a place where death has been destroyed forever.

"We will still grieve. I cannot imagine your pain. But I can promise you that the Lord is good. Even today. Even after this. And he will heal you."

The sky had never looked so far away. I took Crystal by the hand to lead her back to our car, and white shells spilled from her hand.

"I forgot my doves of peace," she said. "I need to give another one to Robby." She cut away from me and ran to the front of the church, against the friends who were filing through the doors to the outside. By the time I reached her, she had already reached up on her tiptoes and placed a white shell in the coffin.

I picked her up and let her head rest on my shoulder. As we made our way to the back of the church, the elusive Ricky Brewer stood erect against the wall, as if someone had pinned his jacket to the white-painted wood. This was the boy who gave my brother his drugs, and now he had the audacity to weep. His eyes were bloodshot and his face blotchy and red.

I wanted to hate him. But my sister squeezed my neck, and it reminded me that he was somebody's brother too. And that meant someone loved him.

I loved my brother. But he couldn't love me because he was gone.

• • • • •

In high school, when a tragedy strikes your family, fame lands upon you for everything that is worst in your life. Victim fame. It was a great irony that I suddenly longed for the days when I was unknown and unloved by my school.

I sat next to Sam in the cafeteria booths and felt the eyes of every student and teacher study me, cautiously, as if I might implode at any moment. Yet somehow none of them seemed to make eye contact. I never caught them staring, but I never felt like they weren't looking. Even Tanya Maldonado found herself speechless. She offered me a shy, closed mouth smile and finished her salad without ceremony.

Mike Lewis told a joke. I forgot to listen. I laughed, but it was delayed. And the sound of it brought the table to a standstill as everyone realized I was faking it. Sam rubbed my hand underneath the table, but I could feel his foot twitching again.

Even at the grocery store, where I thought I could busy myself enough to escape the looming awareness of the Keiser family loss, my customers seemed to know. They pursed their lips and forced smiles across the counter as avocadoes and ground beef passed between us.

I learned that there is no good way to help someone after they've suffered a loss unless they want the comfort. If you ignored me in the hope I would more quickly return to normal, you denied my pain. If you pitied me, you reminded me of my grief. I was angry with the teachers who tilted their heads and wrung their hands. And I was wounded by the classmates who tried to distract me with idle chatter because they somehow thought that thinking about it would be worse.

If I was quiet, they noticed the silence and imagined my pain. If I talked about regular things to distract myself, they saw it as an act. I couldn't hide from what they knew. And, in truth, it felt like a betrayal to do anything but think of Robby. If I held on to my pain, I might just be able to bring him back. And I knew if he could only see us now, he never would have done it. Shouldn't it be that a regret that big could bring a person back to life? He never could have imagined what he meant to us, but that is why he left.

Two weeks after I put my brother into the ground, the dreams came, and one more than others. A faceless man stood at my bedroom door, unflinching as I beat on his chest. "Don't you do it! Don't you do it! How could you?" I believed it was my brother, but I could never see his face to be sure. I only knew I was desperate to get his attention.

It was two in the morning when the sound of my own crying woke me up from a deep sleep. Those are the worst cries of all, when there are so many tears they must spill out of you even when you're not awake.

I walked to the window to eye the moon and saw on the ledge a hibiscus flower, and on its petal the cottage key.

Chapter 13

Sam bounced the white ball off of his forearm and over the net as three boys dove headfirst into the sand to send it back. They failed, and the ball skidded to the side of the makeshift court and into the sea oats that lined the border. Sam grinned at the onlookers who had assembled themselves underneath the perfect blue sky.

Three weeks after I buried my brother, just after finals and before my classmates flowed into the distant corners of summer, Sam convinced me it was time to go out "like normal" again. And so he arranged for a volleyball game at the public beach, where clans from Manatee County high schools would congregate over greasy fries and greedy seagulls and the smell of rich salt water spraying at the shore. This, he said, would be good for me. And he was right, I thought, because how could our hometown paradise refresh me if I never left my room?

The Gulf was a brilliant teal and the sand was a magnificent blazing white that made us squint no matter which way we looked, and it was behind these wrinkled eyes that I could hide the questions I wanted so badly to ask all the kids around me. Were you the last person to see my brother alive? Did you know what drugs he was taking? Did he say anything to you before he went to sleep?

A total of eight different classmates had approached me in the halls my first week back to school to unload their stories of where they saw Robby before he died, and how they thought they saw that faraway look in his eye. But none of these stories gave me the answers I wanted. Every one of them was a reminder of how I had seen that faraway look too. How I had seen it, but didn't respond to it. How I didn't halt my life to check on his. And every story was missing the one thing I needed most: absolution. No one had done everything they could to check on my brother, to stop whatever part of the story they saw play out. Every last one of us let him down. Me most of all. And I would never know what would have happened if one of us had tried.

Sam poured water on my back to shock me into laughing, and I let him have his way for a moment as his friends watched on with ridiculous, hopeful smiles.

"Don't be so quiet," he needled. "Why don't you play some volleyball?"

"With you boys? No way." I pushed a grin his way and shook my head. "I wouldn't want to embarrass you with my superior volleyball skills."

"Aww, come on!"

"No, really. I'm not up for it."

"It'll be good warm-up for tomorrow. Everyone's going to Siesta Key to play against some people from down there, and they're gonna need girls," he argued.

I hated that he had the audacity to speak of the future as if he had a right to it. I wanted Sam to stop the game and even the sunshine in order to hold me like when we were at prom.

"No, thanks," I answered quietly. I looked up to him with pleading eyes. *Please, leave me be.*

"Okay, then." He walked to the other side of the sand court and recruited three long-legged girls to play on his team. They giggled as he insulted his opponents and wondered aloud if there were any risk their bikinis would fall off if he hit the ball just right. One almost went into hysterics when he said, "But if you had to dive for it, I'm just saying there might be a wardrobe malfunction."

It wasn't long before one of the blondes fell, suspiciously gracefully, right on top of him as she dove for a ball that was easily within her reach. The two tumbled in a pile-up of hard abdominals and laughed until one of the boys from beyond the net yelled, "Get a room!"

In his own way, Sam was breaking up with me. I could see it unfolding when he didn't look my way after causing the scene with the other girl. My chest constricted at the thought of losing him too, and I jumped up and yelled for a time-out.

"Uh-oh, Sam. Looks like you're in trouble." Ian spun the ball on the tip of his finger.

Sam hustled over to me with a confident glint in his eye. As he approached, I pulled my hair out of a ponytail, stroked my finger along his chin, and planted a strong kiss on him right on the side of the court. The leggy blondes closed their mouths to hide the shock.

I pulled back just as he reached to pull me closer. "I need to leave, but I want to hang out tonight. Can we go someplace?"

Sam bit his lower lip with a smile. "You got it. My brother's friends are having a party tonight to kick off summer."

Julie, who had stationed herself dutifully by my side during my homecoming, pretended to study her toes.

I turned to her. "Julie, can you give me a ride home? I forgot I need to head over there. Right now." It was all I could do not to break down crying, but I was determined to hold on until we left the beach.

She took a deep breath and grabbed the keys to JP's truck. We headed back to my house. "So, you're going out tonight?"

"Yep." I nodded in a show of confidence that wasn't only for Julie.

"I'm glad. But, Missy, don't you think it might be too soon? I mean, it's okay if you don't go out."

"Julie, what do you want from me? The only time I have fun is when I'm out with you guys." I didn't know why I was yelling at her, but I was too worked up to admit it. I hated being pitied. And I hated the thought of losing Sam. I wanted everything back to the way it had been, when I sparkled in a red dress and had the cutest boy in school looking only at me. I wanted to escape the horrible shadow over my house and forget that nothing was ever going to be the same again. Couldn't Sam save me from all of this just as he had saved me from all my other problems? "I just want to try to do something normal."

"All right, Missy, we'll go out tonight. We'll have fun." She stretched her hand to hold mine and smiled cautiously.

The party was across three bridges into Palmetto, far outside the school district and relative familiarity of the Bradenton neighborhoods, and our connection to it was convoluted. One of Sam's older brothers had scored us the invitation, which likely meant we would know no one else there but him.

Even in the town across the river, Sam was the most popular guy in the room. With an anointing from his big brother, he dominated the crowded room and slapped hands with everyone we passed. JP and Ian trailed behind, uncharacteristically quiet.

"I remember you, man!" Sam shouted at a broad-shouldered guy with a goatee. "Yeah, you scored that Hail Mary in '06. I watched that game!"

I stayed close, clinging to the back of his shirt and overwhelmed at the older girls who didn't look happy to see Julie or me near their men. It didn't matter that they had superior curves or the ability to take control of the room with a flash of their smiles. Julie and I were new, and this made us interesting to everyone who looked our way, which made us a threat. We finally left our dates on the front porch so they could talk about old football games, and we took a seat inside in an almost-forgotten room.

Within an hour, Julie convinced JP to leave, and they offered me a ride home.

"No, thanks." I forced a smile and waved them away. "I should stay with Sam. I'm gonna hang out here."

"Are you sure?" Julie pressed. "It's like thirty minutes to get back home, and Sam's been hanging outside since we got here. I don't think he's in any rush to leave."

I shook my head no. "I told Sam I was going to hang out with him, and I need to do it. I just have to loosen up."

Julie paused as if her hesitation could change my mind. But I wasn't going to leave Sam alone with these older girls. He was the only thing I had going in my life that was actually good. Just weeks ago, I was getting everything I ever wanted, and had confidence because Sam had chosen me. And getting back to that place was the only thing that was going to save me.

"I'm fine. I have Sam here. Really, it's okay." I looked toward JP. "Tell her I'll be fine. Go already."

Julie walked out of the room begrudgingly, and I was left on my own.

I immediately walked to the front porch. Sam wasn't there, but I knew what he needed. He needed to know that I was just as fun as before, and this was the place to do it. No one here knew my story or looked at me with pity. No one here wanted to talk about the last time they saw Robby.

I found an empty seat at a table where a group of guys and girls were playing cards. A thick-looking blond with red stubble on his cheeks ushered me into the circle and taught me the rules of the game.

"So, are you at the community college?" He raised his eyebrows with a charge in his eyes.

"No, um ... still high school."

He rolled his head in disbelief. "Dang! I could have sworn you were a freshman in college." He looked me up and down without trying to conceal it. "You look older."

I swallowed hard. "Thanks."

I played three hands and tried to laugh loud enough at his jokes that Sam would hear me from outside, where I assumed he still was. Maybe he would walk into the room and see that I was still the same person I'd been. Maybe he would see how college boys were paying attention to me.

The blond turned to me and winked. "So, jail bait, what's your name, anyway?"

"Missy."

"Nice to meet you. I'm Rob."

The name startled me, and I sat up straight as the blood left my cheeks.

"You don't like my name? Some people call me Robby if that sounds better to you."

"No, sorry, it's not that." I shot up from my chair and caught my breath. "I'm sorry. I have to go."

I plowed through the crowd to find Sam. Julie was right; this was all too much, too soon. I should have gone home with her. I walked down a long hallway toward the front door. Standing in front of it, Sam was flexing his dimples to one of the blondes from the volleyball court. She was tittering at some remark he made as the two faced each other with their backs against the walls on either side of the hallway. Their shoes pressed against one another's without shame. She looked up first to find me staring.

"Hi!" Her eyebrows raised in surprise.

Sam turned to me and straightened up. "Hey, beautiful. You having fun? This is Becky. She used to go to middle school with us."

Tears began to collect in my eyes, but I choked them back with force.

The girl fidgeted with the belt of her skirt until she finally let the words come out slowly. "Sam was telling me about your brother. I'm so sorry. I can't imagine how hard that must be."

Sam shut his eyes at her words.

"Sorry, I didn't mean to bring it up," she continued. "I just . . . It's really sad. I feel really sad for you, is all."

My bottom lip trembled. She was pitying me, or saying she did, as if it somehow made her look elegant and alive. My hand balled up into a fist instinctively. "And I guess the way you show your concern is by hitting on my boyfriend?"

I don't think I'd ever said anything so rude to anyone's face in my life, but everything inside of me wanted to provoke that girl into a fight.

Her mouth opened in shock. "I don't know what you're . . ."

"Save it. I saw you at the volleyball game today acting all sketchy. Trifling."

The voices on the front porch grew quiet.

Sam stepped between us and placed his hand on my shoulder. "Missy, come on. Don't be like that. Leave her alone."

I hated that I attacked this girl for no good reason. Who was trifling now? I looked up to Sam with fear in my eyes. He was leaving me too. And, in truth, I couldn't blame her for flirting, not when Sam was flashing his dimples and surely giving her some excuse about how he needed to go on a few more dates with me until he knew I was okay. I could see it all clearly now. Those best few weeks in my life were built on a foundation of sand that was now washing out to sea. I had gotten everything I ever wanted when Sam took an interest in me, but it was always meant to be temporary. And it wasn't enough to make me loved.

I turned away in embarrassment at the scene I had created and made my way to the street outside, where a sea of strange cars lined up nose to tail all the way to the main avenue.

Sam followed me to the end of the driveway. "What is going on?"

"Really? She was all over you."

"Look, I haven't done anything with that girl." He pointed to the house as if it were his evidence. "And I thought we were having fun in there. You were, weren't you? Having fun?"

I threw up my hands. "Well, *you* clearly were."

"Don't be like that." He walked toward me and rubbed the side of my arm.

I stared up at him with my mouth half open, but there were no words. Just a few weeks earlier he was trying to convince me we had a special connection to warrant the most special connection of all, and now I was seeing whatever was between us couldn't even weather a summer party.

"I'm sorry, Sam. I really am. I don't want to be one of those jealous girls. I don't even know what I'm doing."

He shuffled his feet to the side and exhaled when he saw the look in my eyes.

I ran my fingers through my hair. "I just don't know if I'm ready to go out yet."

"To parties?"

"I don't know. I guess. It's a lot. Tonight was too much."

Sam pulled a strand of my hair over my shoulder. "My mom was saying you might feel that way. That you're going to need a lot of time."

"Time?" I asked.

"She was saying it's probably going to take awhile for you to get better."

I looked into his eyes, and caught my breath at what I saw. Longing and embarrassment. As if he was telling me he knew exactly what I needed, and he also knew he wasn't willing to give it to me. His place was in a summer party. And he wanted me with him, so long as I was there by his side. I could see that. But he wasn't going to walk away from his life to step into mine. He didn't have the heart to fight for me, and he cared too much to fake it.

Sam's eyes darted to the ground and back to me as if he was searching for words or trying to muster strength that wouldn't come. I could see him floundering; he was in over his head, and knew he couldn't save me even if he wanted to.

I placed my hands on his. I would make it easy for him. "Sam, I'm probably not ready to date right now. I guess we should ... stop, at least for now."

His shoulders dropped with an exhale. I had never seen him look smaller. "I'm sorry, Missy. For all of it. I wish I knew how to make it better."

The relationship I had dreamt of since I was thirteen years old had, for a brief moment, shot into my life exactly as I would have planned it. And I'd discovered that getting everything you always wanted still isn't enough.

Chapter 14

July had come.

But nothing filled the space Robby had left.

Chapter 15

I awoke to another flower on my windowsill, this one a single daisy. Each morning I found one on the white ledge outside my bedroom, and each night it disappeared. Orange blossoms. Marigolds. On one occasion, a magnolia. They served their purpose and were cleared before they could wilt. It was the only secret I can ever remember keeping from Julie, with the exception, at first, of the cottage pool.

I went to her house in the afternoon, where we dodged the summer heat by watching movies on the couch. Her mother set two plates of macaroni and cheese before us, eager to get us out of her house. "Now, what are you girls doing after dinner?"

Julie shrugged and shoveled an orange spoonful into her mouth. "Going out."

I shot her a sharp look. We would not be going out. That was not the plan.

Julie smirked. "On the island. Low key. No biggie."

Mrs. Peterson smiled as she pulled her long, curly hair into a bun. The Florida humidity had turned her locks into an untamable frenzy of blonde frizz. "I remember those days of just going where the wind blew. So fun. Just as long as you're not going to that terrible club in town." She looked down her nose at Julie and me until we squirmed from the guilt. "You know the one I'm talking about?"

"Yeah, Mom," Julie sighed.

"What's it called?"

Julie tilted her head as if pained to say the words. "Club B."

"That's the one. I better not hear about you going there. I'm all for having fun, but you wouldn't believe the stories that are coming out of that place."

The television blared a sitcom until, as if by some cosmic timing, a commercial for Club B began to play.

"Look!" Mrs. Peterson gasped at the screen. "They're advertising that horrible place right now."

The three of us turned to the TV and watched as images from the club filled the screen. Young dancers in tops that were cut too low paraded across the dance floor with ice waters in their hands.

The baritone, super-American voiceover announced: "Club B is the hottest place for Bradenton's fifteen- to twenty-year-olds to dance to the latest hits. Open Friday and Saturday nights, Club B has eight surround-sound speakers and three TVs playing the latest Top 40 music and videos. Don't be the last one to check it out!"

Julie and I tried to hide our smiles as Mrs. Peterson shook her head in disapproval. This was a time when biting my nails might be a good thing. If I didn't cover my face, the woman would surely read my expression and know I was hiding something. And then, just as the commercial was coming to a close, the camera panned around the crowd and zoomed in on a sandy-haired teenager bopping to a beat with a huge, unmistakable smile.

We froze with forkfuls of macaroni hanging out of our mouths.

It was Julie.

She kicked me as the camera zoomed in closer. Not a breath, not a word escaped our mouths as we braced ourselves for the moment Mrs. Peterson recognized her sainted daughter jiggling to the music like a dancer on MTV.

"Well, would you look at that?" She gasped and shook her head with consternation.

We followed her with our eyes as she walked out of the living room and toward the kitchen sink, still talking. "Those kids are obviously much older than you girls, anyway. Despite what that ad claims, college kids are hanging out there."

"Yeah, okay, Mom. We know." Julie's eyes bulged as she called over her shoulder.

The giggles overtook me until I coughed up macaroni into my napkin. I ran to the bathroom for escape. JP would never believe this.

As soon as I opened the bathroom door and entered the hall, Julie pulled on my hand and dragged me to her bedroom. "How did we not see a camera crew around us when we were there? And how on earth is it that we go once, just once, and I'm on some commercial for it?"

Our mouths hung open as laughter squeezed from our lungs. "Shh! Shh! Be quiet! Your mom is gonna hear us!"

"My mother didn't even recognize me! On her own TV! In a close-up!"

It was the first time I had laughed in more than a month, and I did my best to check the voice inside that told me it was a betrayal. No, even Robby would find this hysterical.

Later that night, after we had watched our fill of Molly Ringwald's epic kisses, Julie cajoled me to go to the ice cream shop on the island's north end. The place was the size of a walk-in closet, but it boasted an old-fashioned wooden churn where they made the ice cream with real cream and rock salt. It was pure summertime.

"You know how they get this cookies and cream flavor so good? They literally just pour a box of cookies in it. Nothing artificial." Julie licked the side of her cone and leaned over the railing of the shop's balcony, filled with tables and benches for the patrons to enjoy any breeze. White cream dripped to the parking lot below. She studied my cup of butter pecan. "You should've got a cone."

I shrugged and loaded a spoonful on to my tongue. The flavor wrapped around my mouth in a savory, sweet thickness. It was familiar. Unexpectedly familiar, and too close.

"What's wrong?" Julie rested her hand on my shoulder as my eyes filled with tears.

I shook my head. "I need some water."

She fetched a cup and returned it to me. I had already thrown the dish into the garbage. "I forgot."

"What, Missy? What is it?"

"I'm sorry. I don't mean to be crying."

Old ladies passed us with looks of concern. They walked slowly until Julie waved them away gently.

"I forgot it was Robby's favorite flavor. Just the taste ... it just brought everything back." I laughed and cried through the memories of my brother making me try his ice cream when I was a child. I hated the taste then. I always told him I hated it, and he always told me I wouldn't if I just gave it a chance. I remembered him, pushing a cone to my face with a playful grin. I hadn't even thought about what I was ordering when we entered the shop. But now I wanted to go back to those days so badly, it hurt.

I sat on a bench and wiped my face with paper napkins. "I'm so sorry, Julie. I didn't mean to make a scene. It just hit me so quickly."

She wrapped her arms around my shoulders. "Missy, it's fine. I think that's how this works. Sometimes you're just gonna have to cry."

"He was such a punk!" I laughed again as my eyes cleared. "He used to make my mom buy it every time, even though he knew I hated it. I didn't even realize I'd ordered his flavor, and dang it, if he isn't right. It tastes good."

When I got home, my mother sat with Crystal on the couch, looking awake for the first time since the funeral. She was braiding my sister's hair in a long ribbon down the center of her back, and she patted the seat next to her for me to join them.

I wanted to tell them how I ordered the wrong ice cream, and how I felt like Robby was there with me in that moment. But Crystal wouldn't understand. She didn't have enough time with him to learn these things. And I knew my mother could use a night when the thought of Robby sat next to us, at rest, instead of on top of our chests.

"I'm going to burn off some steam. I'll be out on a bike ride."

"At this hour? But you just got home."

I headed out the door then pedaled as fast as I could. My flip-flops threatened to come lose as my legs rose and fell. Faster and faster. It wasn't long before I reached the docks of the marina, where the light poles were swarmed with moths and other flying things. The boats bobbed in their slips, tied down for the night. Through the sullied shop windows, I could make out a thick figure rummaging through the shelves. I knew it was him, the man who killed my brother.

My breaths came short and heavy. I stood in the parking lot near his SUV, watching him stuff and pull and tuck his things away. Finally, he shut off the light and locked the shop behind him. When he saw me standing on the gravel lot, he swallowed hard.

"Missy." He released a forced, nervous laugh. "I didn't expect to see you out here."

I responded with a blink.

"It's awful late. Shouldn't you be at home by now?"

"I should. But I came to see you." I dug my fingers into the top of my shorts and tried to collect my thoughts. I had him cornered now. Couldn't I make him pay?

I couldn't force this conversation with my mother, who had let my brother down, or my father, who had failed him miserably, like every other adult in his life. Besides, nothing my mother had ever done deserved the loss of her son. In her heart, I knew she loved him more than anyone else on earth. But Bruce I could confront. He only needed to do one thing for my brother, and that was to honor his word. And the greedy thug didn't even do that. He was so embittered by my mother's betrayal that he betrayed Robby as revenge, and cheated him of the boat and his dream. I hated that a lousy boat could have unhinged my brother, but I hated more that this man had taken it from him, with intent.

"Where's the boat, Bruce? Still sitting in the back lot because you needed it so badly?"

"Missy, I don't know what you're doing here, but please."

"You broke your word to my brother."

I was ready for the fight. I would pick up gravel rocks from the lot and pelt him if I had to. I would scream at him until he confessed.

But Bruce didn't fight me. Instead he sagged then staggered to the back of his SUV, propping himself against the back. He held to the sides as he worked to take in each breath.

He placed a hand over his round belly and looked at me as if he was in pain. "I came by your house last week, but your mother didn't think I should see you. I need to tell you how sorry I am for your loss. I am truly sorry about Robby."

My shoulders slumped. The victory I had been hoping to steal from him was gone. It was never there. He was a broken man.

"Missy, if I could take back anything in my life, anything at all from my whole life, I'da never told your brother to move on after your mother and I split. I said horrible things. I was wrong, and I took my frustration with her out on him. I was just so broken that I didn't want to see anything connected to her, but it's no excuse. Missy, I can't sleep at night because I wonder if what I did ... if it pushed him over ... I don't expect you to forgive me, but I want you to know how sorry I am for your loss and that I wasn't better to Robby. He was a good kid. A real good kid. And he deserved better. I shoulda seen that. God, I am so sorry. And if I had known how hard he was going to take it, I like to think I would have ... I'm just sorry that I wasn't better."

I couldn't muster the will to respond. I blamed this man for treating my brother like he was expendable. I wanted to beat on his chest and smear my brother's obituary across his face. But there was no satisfaction in this. Just another broken person.

I went home to settle back into bed as the face of Bruce and the words of his apology sank into my mind. It had been so much easier to blame him for instigating Robby's suicide, and to settle the target of my mind on a man who was no longer in my life. Accepting his apology might put the blame, the relentless blame, back on us, who were with Robby all along—the ones who saw him retreating and heard him question what life was all about but were too busy finding their next man or chasing after the illusion of Sam King.

I awoke in the middle of the night to a wet spray of water landing on my cheek, stirring me from the tenuous sleep I had managed to negotiate with myself. I lifted my head from the pillow and saw Josh's face pressed to the screen with wide eyes. He was spraying me with a water gun.

"I'm sorry," he lied. "Were you trying to sleep?" He stood on the grass in a T-shirt and swim trunks.

I whispered from my bed, "What are you doing out there?"

"You really shouldn't sleep with your blinds up and the window pane open like this. It just invites perverts to come and spy on you while you're passed out."

"That's not funny." I stayed beneath my sheets intent on resisting whatever he wanted to do.

"Come on," he ordered. "We're going out."

I looked to the clock. It was one in the morning and pitch-black outside. "No. I can't, Josh. I don't have it in me."

"Melissa, you can. And I can't let you ignore me anymore."

He was right. I was ignoring him. I wasn't just allowing his flowers to spoil in the sun, I had been ignoring his calls and his visits to the house. On some occasions I would send Crystal to the door to tell him to go away. I didn't even have the courtesy to dismiss him face-to-face. But I knew the only reason he was coming around was out of pity. This was the boy who told me I was all wrong for Sam, the one who seemed to have a problem with everything I did.

"Another night, Josh. I promise."

"No, Missy, tonight. And put on your swimsuit." He stared me down in the darkness. "I'm not leaving without you."

I closed the blinds and changed into a swimsuit and shorts. I plodded to the grass outside with an exasperated thud. "Fine, let's go." I walked toward the cottage, rubbing my eyes from fatigue.

I got ten steps ahead when Josh finally stopped me. "Where do you think you're going?"

I turned around to find him leaning against the side of my house like James Dean. "To the cottage, right?"

"No." The streetlight bounced off of the roof and cast a dark shadow over half of his face, and I couldn't read his expression.

"Well, where?"

He held out his hand in silence until I returned to his side. He led me into his grandmother's Buick and shut the door behind me. When he got into the driver's seat, he turned to me with a furtive smile, his dark eyes tracing the lines of my face to my fingers. He touched my hand briefly.

"Josh, it's been a really hard night."

He pretended not to hear me. "Now, I know you can hardly sit still from the excitement, but I'm not going to tell you where we're going. So don't ask."

"Excitement wasn't the word I was going to use."

He released a small, nervous laugh and drove the car down Gulf Drive, past the motels and the restaurants that were long closed. He drove slowly along the shoreline road, where the cramped Cape

Cod-style beach houses held their stubborn positions between the new complexes that had sprouted around them. Not a soul inside seemed to be awake. Josh clenched his jaw to keep from revealing the surprise. Finally, he turned toward the Gulf and parked his car in front of a home that was marked with high stucco posts and palm trees that reached far above the roof. He pulled the car along the side of the street and parked. He then exited and opened my door for me to follow him.

"Where on earth are you taking us?"

He let a pent-up smile escape and sighed. "Just go with this."

He held my hand and led me around the side of the house, along a narrow path bordered with tall, impenetrable shrubs. When we reached the backyard, I could hear waves from the Gulf crashing just beyond a concrete wall. Josh approached a spiral staircase and began to ascend to the second floor, where there looked to be a patio above.

I whispered for him to stop. "Josh, I can't go up there." Blood rushed to my feet.

"I remember a time when a little trespassing was no different for you than walking down the street. Follow me."

"This isn't a regular house. These people will have us arrested! Someone's going to spot your grandma's car out front. There's no way to run from here."

He tilted his head to patronize me. "Missy, I have everything under control. Can you just trust me?"

"No!"

He laughed. "At least you're honest. Look, I wouldn't put you in a situation that got you in trouble. It's okay that we're here."

I followed him up the stairs begrudgingly and tried to look inside the windows towering above us. I was relieved to see they were completely dark. When we arrived at the top of the staircase, a vast lanai spread out before us. Bamboo couches and potted palms peppered the wooden deck. Josh stepped to the side and allowed me to move across the floor, where a pool stretched out before us, waiting for me, as it reached toward the beach and the night horizon sky.

An infinity pool. The water streamed off of its far side toward the Gulf, and from its elevated height above the sand dunes, I couldn't tell where it ended and the ocean began. A warm, heavy July breeze slipped from the open water and on to the lanai, bringing with it all the electricity of summer.

Josh didn't say a word. I didn't know how he knew it was okay to be there, or why the pool was waiting as if the house were prepared just for us, but it didn't matter anymore. He stepped back against the balcony railing and watched as I walked the perimeter of the pool.

"It's beyond beautiful." I had never seen anything like it. It was almost too wonderful to think I had any right to enjoy it, even if I had owned it. I kneeled beside the stairs and placed my hand in the water. Somehow it was still cool despite the heat around us. I let my hand rest on top of the pool as if to calm its fragile surface.

Finally, I slipped off my clothes down to my bathing suit and slid along the hard surface until I sunk below. Underneath, no one could see me. I couldn't cry and I couldn't breathe. The weight was gone, finally, again.

The world had not given me rest, but here I could steal a moment to myself without its permission. As if the forces that wanted to destroy me had overlooked a loophole. They couldn't find me in the water, where I found respite in the suspension, in free floating above the ground that was holding my brother, above the island that had conspired to keep me from escape. If my lungs hadn't cried for relief, I would have never come up.

And then I swam. Clean, powerful lines waked from my path as I traversed the length of the pool, backward and forward, releasing everything I had. The water readily absorbed whatever I had to give. I lost my breath and held it again. I dove below and glided across the top. When I finally rested, Josh sat at the end of the pool with the outline of tall palm trees framing him from behind.

"You're dancing," he said.

I caught my breath and met his eyes.

He moved into the pool and held my hand gently under the water. "Remember, I know why you like to swim at night, when no one else is around. It's the only place you feel free. It's the only way you know how to escape everything you've been facing."

I looked down to avoid his stare. In the matter of a couple sentences he had expressed something so personal to me that I had never told anyone else about it. "Yes. And if I had the courage, I wouldn't be in a pool at all. I'd be out there, swimming in the Gulf. That's real freedom. Like at low tide when the water is smooth as steel under the moonlight. Sometimes I just want to swim away from here and never turn back."

"Melissa, you don't have to run away or escape to find freedom. This isn't the end of your story. You're still here. And if you can see that, you'd see that being here, right now, is the best thing you can do for Robby."

We looked out to the horizon as the water urged past us and over the edge, and just as I began to feel my heartbeat thump louder at his words, we saw a shooting star trail through the sky and land, it seemed, into the Gulf before us. I tried to exhale. How could I live in paradise and have no peace?

Chapter 16

He was a giant, Viking of a man, memorable for his full gray beard and red hair. He never had a chance at being graceful. And yet, somehow, Josh's pastor wore the ballerina tutu quite well.

"I told you that this wasn't like regular church." Josh's words tickled my ear and a tingle ran through my spine.

That all ended when a brunette with curly, bobbed hair and eyes the color of fog rushed to take a seat by his side. She crossed her legs and clasped her hands to her chest. "Where you been, stranger?" She was beaming at Josh.

I had never seen him smile so broadly. "Working and skimming. The usual."

"Obviously!" She pushed his chest back with a petite hand and leaned over to greet me. "Hi!"

I nodded hello.

"Josh, aren't you going to introduce us?" She tilted her head in curiosity. This girl was too happy. Freckles graced the bridge of her nose like they were angel kisses.

Josh rubbed the back of his neck. Was he nervous? "Jenny, this is Missy. Missy, this is Jenny."

Jenny. Prom date Jenny. Jenny Adams from Cortez Village.

"So, how do you know Josh?" Her eyes fluttered, a trademark display of Southern friendliness.

"We're next-door neighbors, actually."

I saw it register across her face, and the corners of her smile faltered just enough for me to notice. "Oh, right. Really nice to meet you." She nodded, too pleased, too sincere. She knew about Robby. "It's so great to have you here."

"Thanks."

"Well, I'm going to get back, since my things are over there. See you both after?"

I nodded and smiled despite myself. She was too nice to dislike. Too good. My name was probably on some prayer list beside her bed. What was Josh thinking, taking me here?

What was Josh thinking at any rate? He hadn't tried to kiss me or even hold my hand since our night in the infinity pool, but he hadn't left my side in weeks. Even when he was out skim boarding or working with me at the grocery store—after he got a job there too—he managed to leave a flower on my windowsill or a note at my register or a message with my sister. He didn't leave me to the rest of the summer alone. And ever since we saw our shooting star, I didn't try to fight him anymore. If Josh wanted me to go to church with him, I would sit through and bear it, if only to pay him back for everything he was doing for me. He was the only thing keeping me out of my room whenever I wasn't working or Julie was around, and the only one who could help me feel as if I had escaped, if only for a minute at a time.

Pastor Bill removed his tutu when the skit was finished and the laughter in the room died to a quiet mumble, leaving a certain warm energy in the air. He asked everyone to take a seat.

Josh's eyes flickered with the look of expectation. I had finally agreed to attend youth group. I forced a smile and looked his way. *I'm here. I hope this makes you happy.*

I mashed my lips together and surveyed the room. The kids around us weren't my usual friends. They were the anonymous faces, the ones who sat in the middle of the bus or in the front of the football bleachers. They had probably never been the target of Tanya's inquisitions or given a second look to Sam King's cafeteria booths, because they weren't on anyone's radar.

Josh's elusive prom date, Jenny Adams, leaned against a wall, eyes bright. Was she as aware of me as I was of her?

Pastor Bill interrupted my thought. "Right now my wife is pouring a pitcher of water."

A cheerful woman half his size brought a glass pitcher to the stage and set it on a stool beside him. I braced for the lecture.

The pastor raised the container. "What if I told you that this water was not just any water? What if I told you that it came from the freshest, purest ice glacier in the Arctic Circle? We personally shaved the ice from this glacier and let it melt in a perfectly clean, crystal container, and brought it down here to the island where it was certified as the purest form of water anyone had ever seen. Completely untainted by all of the chemicals we have in our water today. What if I told you that we could all have a glass to drink? Would you like some of that water?"

He pulled out an empty glass and poured from the pitcher. He held it up to the light as it refracted rainbows of color. "But what if, before we drank it, my wife came back and she put in a small portion of lethal toxic waste? And what if this was not just any waste, but radioactive fallout taken from one of the most polluted sites in all the earth? The kind that brings the worst kind of death."

Pastor Bill's wife returned to the stage and emptied a few drops of liquid into the glass. It dotted the surface of the water and then disappeared below.

"Would it be okay if I drank from this glass now?"

He held the contaminated water to his lips. I squirmed at the sight.

"Or, what about you?" He held out the glass of water to a girl in the front of the room. "Could I give you a drink from this glass? Come on now, what if I mixed it in real well?" The girl waved her hands away, and he laughed at her reaction. "You won't even take the glass, and you know it's only pretend!"

The room giggled at the thought.

"There's a philosophy out there that states that if you do enough good in life, it will outdo all the bad you do. But that belief actually has nothing to do with what God teaches. The Bible tells us that we're like that glass of pure water, created to be close to God. But along the way, each of falls short of what we were intended to be, of God's perfect, holy, and pure grace. Every single one of us has messed up. And just like with my glass here, just a little bit of our sin—of contamination that comes from mistakes we make—pollutes the whole body. That is because we were intended to be in fellowship with God, to be in his company of absolute purity and love and peace. And when we step away from that, it's like we're choosing instead to take poison."

I shifted a little when his eyes turned to my side of the room. How much did he know about me?

"Now, if you're God, and you love your children beyond all measure, you want them back even if they're poisoned. You don't want to give up on them. But you can't pretend the poison isn't there, either. You want to make your children's glasses—their souls—pure again.

"If you see yourself in this glass of water, and you know you have made decisions that make you less than pure, take comfort. Realizing that fact is one of the most important moments in your life. Because when you see sin for what it does and how it harms you and the people around you, you have the opportunity to ask God to step in and make you pure again. The Bible says, 'Yet to all who did receive him, to those who believed in his name, he gave the right to become children of God.' He has created a way for you to come back home and be in relationship again. Nothing you have done can separate you from his goodness. And the best news of all, he has already made the way. You just have to ask."

The room was silent. Not even Josh dared to look my way. I could feel the tears breach the barriers of my eyelids as I thought of what my glass would be. If I lived a perfect life and failed my brother, it was enough to poison me forever.

I rose from the group and made excuses to go to the restroom. When I got inside, I felt my lungs collapse within me, and the desperate sense that I would always feel alone suffocated me from the inside. Josh entered and stood next to the sink. His eyes were soft.

"You shouldn't be in the girl's room, Josh."

He crossed his arms in defiance. "Well, neither should you right now. Are you okay, Missy?"

"I saw a look in his eyes, Josh." The tension released from my shoulders. It was the first time I said it out loud. "I knew something was wrong when I left Robby at prom. And I left anyway because I wanted to go off to a party. I wanted to feel beautiful, and I left him. It was the ugliest thing I've ever done in my whole life."

Somewhere behind him a faucet was dripping, and the ping of water echoed off of the tile walls. Everything I was feeling seemed to be magnified.

"Missy, I know if I tell you it wasn't your fault, you won't listen to me."

"No, I won't. And it's not just me, Josh. Everyone failed him. Our so-called dad. Our mom. Bruce and that stupid boat. It's like we were all sleeping on the job. Everyone failed. And Robby too. He had no right to do this to us."

"You need to hear me now. Whatever guilt you feel, whatever you did or failed to do, God saw it all, and he'll find a way to make you whole again. That's what grace means. Jesus is not just for the small stuff."

I couldn't bear to hear these things, and I'd never dreamed Josh would be the one spouting them. "I don't deserve forgiveness. You have no idea how much I don't deserve it."

He walked toward me. "That's the whole point, Melissa. We don't deserve it. That's why we need grace."

I felt the roughness of his hands wrap around mine, and though I didn't welcome the exact words he said, suddenly I felt closer to him in that moment than all the times I had been in Sam's arms.

• • • • •

The last slow days of summer provided distraction, somewhere between the beach with Crystal, and working at the grocery store, and Josh's failed attempts to teach me to skim board. When I was doing something, I wasn't thinking of my brother or how I could have stopped him.

No one went into his room. We shut the door and kept the dirty clothes unwashed. Sometimes I would hear my mother step inside, breathe deeply, and return to her bedroom.

When Josh made the mistake of buying a stick shift pickup truck, I had something new to learn, something new to do. It was red and had a clutch and a drive shaft and all sorts of equipment I had no idea how to use. Not to mention my driving skills were a little rusty—I hadn't driven since we got back from Pennsylvania, since Denise always had the car.

"You have to let me learn! You have to teach me!" I folded my arms in a show of protest.

"No way! It's a brand-new truck, and you'll ruin the transmission." He shook his head wildly and raised a hand as if to block out the sight of me.

"Brand new? It's a ninety-seven!"

"Brand new to me. That's all that matters." He stomped around the truck with a rag and buffed off a coat of wax.

"Oh, puh-leeze, Josh!" I pulled the baseball cap off of his head and tried to pull the keys out of his hands.

"No way!" He wrestled to get away from me until his grandmother came out of the house to see about the commotion.

"Joshua, whatever that darling girl wants from you, you better give it to her." Mrs. Durham always was a reasonable woman.

For some reason, Mrs. Durham hadn't returned to Michigan to escape the Florida heat, as usual, and at some indeterminate point in the last month my status with her had been officially upgraded from pool trespasser to darling girl. I stood straight with my mouth open in smug satisfaction. "I think you should listen to your grandmother, Joshua."

He shook his head. "Most annoying girl in the world. You."

"Excellent! Annoying wins in the end!" I announced and plopped myself into the driver's seat.

He came to the driver's window with an incredulous look across his face. His eyebrows scrunched up in disbelief. "You don't actually think you're going to be driving right out front here, do you? We're going to need to take this to a parking lot and give you some room so you don't accidentally hit something."

"How hard can it be, Josh? It's already parked on the side of the street. I just have to drive straight."

"Missy, you have no idea how to drive a stick, and this doesn't even have automatic steering. Do you have any idea what that means?"

I shook my head slightly as if the point he was raising couldn't possibly matter. "Just give me the keys and get in. I'm going to be great at this. You'll see."

He walked around to the passenger side of the truck and mumbled under his breath, "I just want you to know that this goes against everything I want to do."

He pointed to the parts I'd need to know. The clutch was the leftmost pedal. The shift would need to be thrown into the bottom right in order to move in reverse. He made me practice with the ignition turned off. And, finally, once I assured him I was a natural, he sat back in the seat and put on his seat belt.

"I've got this. You told me you learned in a day. So can I, right?"

Josh rubbed his forehead. "One try. That's it. Then, *when* you stall, we'll go to a parking lot."

I turned on the ignition, punched in the clutch, swung the shift to first gear, and applied the gas. At first the engine revved but we didn't go anywhere because I forgot to release the clutch. Then I tried it again. Clutch out, gas in. The truck jolted forward. I gassed it. Success! And then an abrupt, violent stop.

I turned to him with my eyebrows scrunched to my forehead. "That didn't feel like just a stall."

"It wasn't."

We stepped out of the truck to assess the damage. In front of the bumper, wedged underneath the front right tire, his grandmother's manatee-shaped mailbox was flattened on the asphalt. The fat, gray sea cow was squashed by Josh's truck into a heap of plastic and metal.

My shoulders scrunched to my ears as I braced for his reaction.

"You whacked my grandmother's manatee." He bit his bottom lip and turned to me, nodding slightly.

"Oh, Josh. I'm so sorry. I'm so, so sorry."

He shook his head in dismay. "I can't fix this. It's flattened." He picked up the manatee's plastic tail in his hands. It was folded in two. "Don't you know these are an endangered species?"

A short laugh escaped my mouth in relief.

"I mean, poor guy didn't see what was coming. And he never hurt anyone. Just spent his life out here by the street collecting mail. Oh, such a sad way for a manatee to go. Smushed by a crazy teenage driver. What would Robby say . . ."

He tried to stop himself the moment my brother's name escaped his lips, but it was too late. He had done what I had done a thousand times that summer — forgot that my brother was actually gone and not just out skim boarding somewhere, late for dinner.

I smiled at him warmly. "Robby would say it was your fault for letting me drive."

Chapter 17

It was late August, and Mrs. Durham's mailbox had been reduced to a plain, metal bin on top of a wooden post. Very un-island. We had still not replaced the shattered manatee. This was because Mrs. Durham refused to take cash from me, or her beloved grandson who made the mistake of allowing me to drive his truck. No money. She preferred favors — sweat equity.

The job was fairly simple this errand. Josh and I were to load up the back of his truck with spare folding chairs and take them from the garden club to the senior citizens center. He would drive. From what I gathered, island retirees were planning a USO-themed reception, modeled after the Korean- and World War II-era socials that American small towns hosted for returning soldiers. It meant swing music and rosy-cheeked widows and bald men in VFW ball caps. And they invited veterans from Iraq and Afghanistan too, although only one or two would show up. It was the talk of the island's seniors, and it was to begin at four that afternoon, which was late enough, after all.

The simple task turned into two hours of hard labor, but who could say no to senior citizens who pinched your cheeks and asked you to call them by their first names, like Mabel and Dolly?

Whenever I saw Julie, she told me she was glad Josh had become a good friend, but she was confused by what he wanted. I had spent nearly every day with him for the last month.

"I just wish you would hang out more like you used to. What is he up to, anyway? I don't know a lot of guys who would spend that much time with a girl and not want her as his girlfriend. I mean, he never tries to kiss you?"

After she raised the questions a third time and didn't get anywhere—because I had no answers—she agreed to drop it. And so I embraced the chance to run Mrs. Durham's errands. It meant more time with Josh, and more distraction from the bigger questions that still loomed over my house and occasionally haunted my dreams.

Josh and I unloaded the folding chairs and helped Ms. Mabel hang streamers from the high ceiling. She draped a banner that read, "Welcome home, boys!"

Old men tugged on Josh's arm and lectured him about how today's dancing is a losing proposition. "We don't understand you kids today. Why dance apart from each other when you can be dancing hand in hand, cheek to cheek? You really lost out on that one."

Josh conceded the point.

When a five-piece band settled into the front of the room, I shook Josh's shoulder and explained we couldn't leave.

"It's a real band! With horns!"

"Missy, this event is for senior citizens. I don't think we're really welcome here. And if any of these people knew what you do to manatee mailboxes, you can be sure we'd be kicked right out."

"I'm willing to take my chances."

He eyed the room. There were more old women than men, and we both knew that would mean indentured servitude for one of us. Mrs. Durham would promise a dance with her grandson to anyone who complimented her on what a nice young man he seemed to be. Which clearly wasn't an ideal afternoon for a surfer with brooding eyebrows. "Outside. Now. Before it's too late."

He took a seat on the park bench outside the center and turned away to keep from making eye contact with me. "I'm not looking at you, because I know you're going to make me go in there, and there's no way that's happening."

"Please, Josh! I want to see if you can keep step with Ms. Dolly."

He shook his head, fighting a smile. But he wasn't budging. "No. We're waiting here until my grandma lets me know she's done with us. And then we're gone. And we're done with all free labor. We probably earned that mailbox days ago."

I took a seat next to him on the bench. Pieces of my hair stuck to my neck from the humidity, and I sighed at the heat. "It's really hot out here."

"That isn't working on me." He smiled begrudgingly and shook his head. "Anyway, we're in shorts. We're not dressed for it."

I nodded my head in disbelief. It was the first time I had ever heard Josh concerned with clothing. Music escaped through the doors, and seniors walked past us and into the building, breaking into smiles at the blare of the horns. I wondered how they could smile at the sound of days they could never get back, but I supposed that enough time had gone by that all they could remember now were the smells, and the steps, and the laughter, and had somehow made peace with the people they had lost. Pink floral dresses and blue plaid pants paraded by.

Ms. Dolly walked by with a plate of cookies in her hand. She practically tutted at us. "Now, what are you two doing outside? The party is just starting."

"*Josh* doesn't want to go in." I crossed my arms with satisfaction. Ms. Dolly was a New Yorker. It wouldn't take much to get her going.

"That's a shame, dear, because a USO dance is something you don't want to miss. That's music from Glenn Miller you're hearing in there. Best music there ever was, in my opinion."

The jump of the horns rattled through the walls. It was just as good as any beat I heard at prom.

"I'm not going to force you, but it is quite an event to see. Some of those fellows in there are World War II vets, some Korea. When they got home, we held these dances for them. That's what you do when you have someone go out and save you and you have no way to repay them back for all they've done. Sometimes the only thing to do is celebrate." Her eyes misted and she headed to the building. If that didn't break Josh's resolve, I don't know what else would.

He sat quietly and tapped his foot. I knew I could outlast him on this, and before long the heat would drive us inside. Or maybe the rain.

The storm arrived with no warning. Clouds rushed overhead and thunder beat off the sides of homes as flashes of white lightning lit up the sky. Florida storms came in an instant. Water tumbled down on to us from the sky and ran down our hair.

"I guess we're going inside." Josh grinned and took my hand. "But let's go in the back. At least give me a chance at hiding."

I followed him in through a side door that landed us at the far end of the party, in the shadow of a long metal divider. If we took a few more steps, we'd be in the center of the room, fully visible. But beside the back door, under the coolness of the air conditioning vent, we stood in our personal cubby.

Voices and laughter echoed around us. And then the band started to play again, and the whole crowd began to talk to each other in sentimental tones. It was a slow melody, a sweeping, sleepy song.

Josh turned to me, wiping the last bits of rain off of his face. "It's 'Moonlight Serenade.'"

"How do you know the name of this song?"

He smiled. "I'm Mrs. Durham's grandson, remember?"

He clenched his jaw in concentration and lifted my hand against his, then rested his other hand on my waist. Before I could fully process what was happening, he stepped closer, until I felt his warm breath against my forehead, and he swayed. Left. Right. Closer. He moved his arm to the small of my back, and I rested mine on his shoulder. I felt the dent of his collarbone against my chin and his chest inhale and release. We were dancing.

When the song ended, I heard Mrs. Durham call with delight, "Joshua, you came inside after all."

We looked up to see her standing with a tray of pink lemonade. Jenny Adams was by her side, mouth open in surprise, wearing a summer dress that made her look like a poem.

"Jenny's here to help with the refreshments." Mrs. Durham pointed to the back door. "Here, Jenny, you prop this door open so the other boys can bring in some ice."

I noticed Mrs. Durham knew her well enough to call her by name. Josh dropped my hand and stepped to the side. He opened the door so Jenny could get by.

The dance was over.

• • • • •

Sand dunes rose around us like puffy clouds of baking flour. Bean Point wasn't a place where we gathered often, but tonight a throng of teenagers collected where the northern tip of the island saluted the bay and observed the currents rushing in from the Gulf.

Julie insisted this was a party I couldn't miss. She had too many questions that needed answers, and I tried to muster the same excitement for them, anything to feel normal. Who had gotten hotter? Who had started a summer fling? These things need to be settled as our class returned to school and tried to find its old, familiar groove again, this time for the last time. This time as seniors. I knew from past experience there would always be a few who stumbled, a few of the familiar pieces that suddenly refused to fit into the old molds. Maybe that was Josh and me.

Scores of people descended upon the beach. Some strummed guitars and others lay on oversized blankets. It was harder to have gatherings after dark during tourist season. But in the last stretch of the hot months, the island was left to the locals and most of the adults were trapped inside their air-conditioned homes. Self-imprisonment. With most of the vacationers gone, there were fewer adults to be bothered, and the police could rest in knowing they could name nearly everyone who crossed their paths.

Leigh took a seat next to me and tied her hair into a messy bun to keep the heat away. "Where you been all summer, Missy? We've missed you."

"Oh, around. I've been hanging out with Josh a lot, actually. And working a bit."

"Josh Durham? I just saw him on Bridge Street. He was walking with some brunette. Is he coming tonight?"

I swallowed hard. "No, he couldn't make it."

Josh had told me he needed to work a late shift, not that he was hanging out with Jenny Adams. Could he be dating her? Is that why her mouth hung open when she saw us dancing? Maybe we were only friends.

I thought of her curly hair and piercing gray-blue eyes. She had a glow around her. And—more than that—she was good. She sat in church like she belonged. Of course Josh was dating her, and saving me from knowing so I wouldn't be hurt.

He had to work? He had been working a lot lately. Maybe he wasn't getting more hours than me—maybe he was off romancing Jenny. Did it count as lying if he was only doing it out of pity?

I tried to clear my head of the thought.

"There she is. Hey, stranger."

My eyes chased the voice that came from beside me. Bare feet, muscular legs, board shorts, and then, finally, dimples. "Sam."

He stood over me with a smile that still could hitch my breath.

"You look great, Missy," Sam said.

He reached for my hand with an easy confidence, bronzed from a summer of football practice.

I took his hand to stand and smiled weakly in return. "Hey, Sam." It was the first time I had seen him since we broke up.

"I mean it. Somehow you've gotten even prettier." His eyes twinkled as he got close enough to hug me hello. "So, what have you been up to?"

I looked away. Was he really asking me this? "Not much."

"Well, whatever you're doing, it's working for you." He took a strand of my brown hair and twirled it around his finger. "Let's go down to the water and catch up."

He had gotten even taller and stronger looking, and I could feel the old need to be with him start to bubble up as he got closer. I resented that I still felt the old crush for him. But somehow it was hollow this time. Instead, my mind was filled with images of Josh sitting with Jenny on the Bridge Street swings.

I placed my toes in the water. "And how about you? What are you up to?"

"Missing you." He answered without a moment's pause. "I've missed you a lot."

"I've missed you too, Sam." I felt like a parrot, repeating his words back to him with little thought. I suppose I did miss him in some way. Things were simpler when we were together, when my brother was here.

"Look, Missy, I know you needed your space, but I've really been looking forward to seeing you again. I'm glad I ran into you tonight. Maybe it was supposed to be. So I'm just going to say it. I want you back."

He reached for my hand. He was clear about what he wanted, unlike Josh. Also unlike Josh, it seemed, he wanted me. I never knew if I was the girl of Josh's dreams or a little sister to him. I thought of

Jenny's bright smile, how sweet she was to me though she must have known how I felt. Could I ever be like her?

Sam pulled my hand closer. "Haven't you missed this?"

"I don't ..." I stumbled to find words. "I don't think ..."

Maybe Julie was right. Maybe Josh would have made a move on me by now if he liked me. Josh simply felt sorry for me.

Sam continued, "I'm saying I want another chance with you." He leaned toward me and placed his hand on the back of my neck. He pressed his lips to mine tenderly, and I felt my lips kiss him back.

Nothing in me wanted to be this close to him. But isn't this where I belonged? He placed both hands on my cheeks, and I could tell he was kissing me with everything he had. Seconds passed, and I waited for the old feelings to come back in full force. But it wasn't enough. It wasn't real. It wasn't Josh.

I pulled back. "Sam, I'm sorry. I just can't get back together with you."

"What? Don't you want to?" He seemed shocked.

"No, I'm sorry. I'm not the same girl I used to be."

The old Missy would have swooned in his arms. But not now. I hadn't allowed myself to think about my feelings for Josh until tonight, as if enjoying him would betray my grief. Each day Josh woke me up at one in the morning to go swimming or dragged me from the couch to head down to the surf, I told myself that all I needed to feel was gratitude I had a friend. But I had been fooling myself, because deep inside I had been feeling much more, things I hadn't even realized until Sam held me on the beach. I was supposed to like Sam. That is who I was. But being in his arms felt like a counterfeit.

Sam had tried to love me, in his own way. But he never could because he loved himself more.

And now that I realized that Josh was what I wanted, I had to consider that he might not want me. I might not be good enough for him, in the truest sense of the words.

I left Sam and returned home to recount all that Josh had done for me, how any average girl would have construed the summer we spent together. Wasn't every kindness an invisible contract between us, a promise that one day I would be his girlfriend? Weren't there realities at hand, even if the words weren't there? And what was I supposed to do with all this information? If he was dating Jenny now, could I pretend he was nothing more to me than a friend?

I needed to know. Suddenly, the need was immediate. I wanted him to fight for me; not to ease my pain, but to make me his.

I waited for him at the cottage pool that night, but he didn't show.

I waited for him the next day after our shifts were done at work, but he didn't come by.

I peered out my window to see if I could tell when he got home, but I never saw his light turn on.

Finally, I sat on the front lawn and played with Crystal until he finally came outside.

Josh walked with a heaviness toward his truck. He threw his skim board into the bed and looked the other way when I turned to see him. The sight of him made my stomach drop.

"Josh, hey."

"I can't talk right now, Melissa." His dark eyes flashed to me for a split second as if in search of mercy.

"Where have you been?"

"I've been busy. I'll catch up with you later."

I stepped toward him through the grass. "Come on. How busy can you be? I haven't seen you all week."

He left me standing in the yard as he pulled away. His jaw was clenched tight as he shifted through the gears and sped on to the main road.

He didn't come to his door that night after dinner. And he didn't answer his phone when I called. There was a weirdness between us that I didn't understand. It had arisen suddenly and deprived me of the chance to find out if what I thought about Jenny was true. How could I make him sorry he didn't choose me if he wasn't even talking to me?

I left a note on his bedroom window ledge, but he let it soak in the rain. The truth was that there had hardly been a day since I returned to the island that didn't begin and end with the knowledge that Josh Durham would be there for me. Even when I hated knowing it, he was a constant in my life. And even when I lost my brother, Josh didn't let up. I had never before felt the sure, solid feelings for him that began to uncover themselves when he started to withdraw. He had moved into my heart, and all this time I thought I had a vacancy. The truth is I was aching to be near him, even if that only meant friends. I could have dated twenty other Sam Kings, but none of them would make me feel as loved as when I was near Josh.

Days passed. Fear that he might not choose me transformed into anger that he didn't. And worse yet, it seemed to mean that I was going to lose him even as a friend. What had I done?

Josh was shutting me out, and there wasn't enough time to understand why. A storm was on its way.

In Florida, hurricane season is left to the locals to handle. The tourists have all left by the time the great storms work their way into a circular fury across the south Atlantic or up from the Caribbean. And every native has their storm story to tell, a mixture of defiance and awe that ends with an accounting of what they lost or what lesson they gained.

At the grocery store, women with their hair in loose buns made a run on batteries and bottled water while their husbands purchased plywood to cover their bay windows. In the lead up to the hurricane that came to the island that year, Florida residents saw a cloud mass that yielded wind gusts of one hundred ten miles per hour and realized there was nowhere to go.

The storm's fury was destined for counties four hours to the southeast. And by the time it would sweep across the everglades and charge upward toward the Gulf, it would lose the fury that could peel back rooftops and toss sailboats on to dry land like Frisbees. Which meant the forecast for Anna Maria was, by comparison, a rude hangover of the beast, and we knew it. Relatives from out of state called to report that dangerous winds and rains were headed for Manatee County as if they had access to news that our own forecasters were too afraid to share. But the locals knew that the fight we'd face was a lightweight compared to our sister communities.

We could expect a curfew, and flooded streets, and the hoarding of clean water, and a long day and night of power outages. But that was nothing compared to what would happen elsewhere. And this is what the islanders told themselves as the sea turned to a curious, flat plane and the smell of something humid and electric filled the air. Landfall would begin around midnight, the forecasters said. And, until then, we could do nothing but wait.

"We're closing the store early," my boss ordered. "Pull in everything from outside. Move the glassware away from the windows, and let's shut down as soon as we can."

I had never worked so quickly. Josh was nowhere to be seen. For some reason, we hadn't worked the same shifts for a while. Was he trying to avoid me? I thought about asking my boss about Josh, but just went home instead. When I arrived, Crystal and Denise were counting jars of chicken noodle soup, grabbing the camp stove, and pulling out candles from storage.

"It's gonna storm tonight," Crystal announced with worry. Since Robby had passed, threats were no longer adventures. They were real. Her childlike excitement about the unknown was extinguished.

"Yes," Denise said. "But we talked about how the big part of the storm is not coming to the island."

I rubbed my sister's shoulder. "That's right. Our storm is just going to mean a bunch of rain. Nothin' much."

"Then why is Mrs. Durham going?" Crystal pointed out the front window.

She was right. Josh's grandmother was rolling a piece of luggage to the backseat of her Buick. Josh was nowhere to be seen.

I rushed out of the house and called to Mrs. Durham, "How are you? Is everything okay?"

"Yes, dear. Are you all doing well?" She shut the back door to her car and looked to the sky. "This is the price for living in paradise this time of year. It's all to be expected."

"Yes, ma'am." I nodded. "Are you evacuating? I understand they're doing some voluntary evacuations, but it's not mandatory yet."

"Well, I'm headed in town to stay with Josh's dad. I haven't been through many of these storms before, and I suppose I'd rather be with my son than out here on the island. I'm trying to head out before they shut the bridges down."

I tried to look past her and into the dark windows of her house to find an outline of Josh. He couldn't possibly ignore me while I was standing on his driveway talking to his grandmother.

"We'll be back in a couple of days, I'm sure." She studied my worried face and smiled gently. "Josh isn't here right now, dear. He's gone to help Pastor Bill with his boat. Bill's been visiting family up north this past week, and so Josh went by to check on it."

"Oh, I see. Well, travel safe. Feel free to call if you need us to check on anything at the house."

"Thank you, Missy. We will. At least I don't have to worry about whether my mailbox will survive the storm." She winked. "And, you know ... Josh just left a few moments ago. I'll bet he's there right now."

Chapter 18

Anna Maria was small; for the most part we all knew of each other. So even before I'd met Pastor Bill, I was aware he lived on the canal side of Holmes Beach, on a street where a boat could float off of the backyard dock. Thanks to the island gossips, everyone knew he had inherited the place from his parents, and he could have turned a pretty profit by selling it during the boom and moving in town. But he stayed on the island, leaving some folks, like my mother, to wonder out loud if his church salary covered the hurricane insurance and the taxes. I kissed Crystal good-bye and set out for the place on my bike.

The neighborhoods had shrunk to a skeleton crew, and I didn't pass a single car on my ride up Bill's street. The families that chose to evacuate had fled to the mainland earlier in the day. The pastor's house looked dark and empty. Aluminum hurricane shutters were rolled over the larger windows and buckled down to protect the glass. Rings of brown dirt stained the concrete walkway to the front door. The potted plants had been taken inside before the storm, most likely along with the garbage cans and the porch furniture.

I ran to the side of the house and called over the backyard fence, working to catch my breath. "Josh! Josh! Are you there?" I wasn't going to be ignored for another minute.

Between the high brown planks, I could make out the flashes of movement at the far edge of the yard, where the canal bordered the backs of the homes.

"Josh!"

If he heard me calling, he wasn't going to budge.

The house to my right had no fence blocking the way to its backyard, and there looked to be no one home. I ran on the neighbor's grass, alongside the pastor's border to the far back of the yard, until I reached the seawall. The end of the fence jetted out just over the salt water. If I held on to the post, I could swing my body over the water and around the edge of the fence to land in the pastor's backyard. *One ... two ... three.*

I landed right foot first. I used the fence to pull myself erect and gathered the rest of my body around the side. I looked up. Josh was staring at me with disapproving eyes, perched on top of a boat with a wrench in his hand.

"Trespassing? At a pastor's house? You can't help yourself, can you?"

I shrugged awkwardly and walked toward the dock as he returned his attention to the vessel's motor.

Josh was gorgeous in the gray light of the pre-storm dusk. Oil marked his forearms and the humidity washed his skin in a cloudy glow that reminded me of the first time he spoke to me at his grandmother's pool.

He hustled about the deck to turn switches and test the ignition as if my arrival meant nothing to his work. "Why are you here, Melissa?"

"To see you."

"Lucky me." He looked to the deck and shut his eyes briefly, as if he was fighting to keep uglier words from escaping. "Sorry."

"We need to talk, Josh. You can't just ignore me."

He released a dismissive smile and twisted the wrench around one of the greasy plugs at the back of the boat. "Missy, I'm sorry

I haven't been around in a while. I'll catch up with you after this storm. But right now I have to get this boat working."

"Why can't you wait to fix it until after the storm? Let's just cover it up and get back home." I had him cornered now, and I wasn't going to let him go without confronting him.

He balanced himself on the boat as it remained tethered to the dock, bobbing slightly. His fingers tensed on the wrench. Orphaned wires crisscrossed in front of him, clearly in need of more of his attention. "I don't have time right now. I'll be done here in a second, and then I'm pushing off."

"Pushing off? What are you talking about?"

Josh kept his head down. "I have to get it up the river and dock it somewhere safer. Don't worry about it."

"That's madness. The storm's gonna be here any moment now."

"I have a few hours. If I don't get it out of here now, the storm surge will hit the boat and ruin her." He shot me a sharp look through the corner of his eyes. "I have enough time if people don't get in my way."

"Josh, I know your pastor wouldn't want you to go to this amount of trouble for him. And this boat doesn't even look that new. I'm sure he'll understand if you couldn't get it out of here in time. Let's just go home."

Josh wiped his forehead with his arm, swiping a faint mixture of sweat and engine grease across his hairline. "Look, I'm going to dock her up the river, and my dad is going to pick me up from there. I'll come around and talk with you in a few days, once I'm back on the island."

Anger burned in my chest. "What is up with you? Are you tired of hanging out with me or something? You have a new charity case? Just let me know, and I'll leave you alone, I promise."

He clenched his jaw. "You don't want me to answer that question right now, trust me."

"Any answer would be better than what you've been giving me. I just don't know why you haven't talked to me in over a week. And if that's no big deal to you then just say so."

"No big deal," he answered dryly.

His words punched me in the gut. Just before he looked away to fidget with the plugs, I saw a glimmer of fear in his eye and his bottom lip drop open just a bit to catch his breath.

The seagulls flew with violence as the horizon grew to a deep gray. Premature darkness slowly set in over the sky, and a hush swelled up from the island. Only the angry creaks of the boat and the call of the birds circling above dared to make any noise now.

Josh rose from his work and looked up with resolve. At the captain's chair, he started the engine. "I'll call you later."

He wasn't bluffing. He was going to leave without me. He leaned over the bow and untied the boat from the first post, then the others. He was just seconds from pushing off.

Something inside me knew that if he left me there, alone in the pastor's backyard as a hurricane headed for our town, we would have both passed an invisible line. Something irreversible would creep into that safe place between us, in the distance between our bedroom windows, where he left clues and I left footprints. I couldn't let him leave like this. And, most of all, I needed to know why it was that I got so close to getting it right with him but had come up just short. I was going to make him tell me. I bolted across the dock and jumped on to the deck as the boat cleared its mooring.

"What do you think you're doing?" He raised his hands in protest as the boat drifted sideways from the brown dock. The engine rumbled low in idle.

"I'm going with you if that's what I have to do. I'm not going to be set aside anymore."

"Melissa, no."

I sat down into the co-captain's chair and clung to the seat with resolve. He could see the fury on my face, and I knew that we both understood he would not be able to make me leave the boat without removing me with brute force, something he would never do. By the time he won the fight, he'd miss his window and the storm would arrive. He was going to get off the boat, or he was going to take me with him.

"I'm not playing, Missy. If you head up the river with me, you might not be able to get back to the island in time. These roads are going to wash out and they'll close the bridges."

"I'll figure something out. It's only one night."

Josh closed his eyes in frustration, as if he was praying for an angel to save him. "Get. Off."

"Come. Home."

He stared me down, willing me off his boat, but I refused to blink. Then, finally, he exhaled in defeat.

"Fine. You're on your own once we get in town." We headed down the long canal in stubborn silence as neighbors placed sandbags along the backside of their houses.

After rounding the last house of the canal, we pulled into the bay, where the water was smooth and thick, like a vat of mercury. The hum of the old engine groaned in a rhythm of peaks and valleys, leaving an eerie calm to simmer between us.

The houses along the island's inland coast grew smaller as we moved north, farther away from land and past the northern tip of Anna Maria, where the southern mouth of Tampa Bay and the western gate of Manatee River conspired to form a ghost of a triangle whose points were connected by nothing more than seawater and invisible currents. It had grown dark too quickly, and the boat offered only a small light on its bow to guide us. Josh steered slowly to avoid the sandbars that could run us aground at low tide. I stayed quiet as he headed for the shipping lane. He was still doing his best to ignore me.

"I want you to sit up by the bow and make sure nothing is in our way. I don't want to hit ground or anything like that." He gestured to the front of the boat.

I complied and took a new seat, where the two sides of the boat met in an arrow tip. These were normally crowded waters, filled with crab boats and sailboats. But the channel was empty tonight, its captains dry-docked, no doubt counting the hours with a grudge. "We're the only ones out here."

Josh looked out of the corner of his eyes. "Yeah, well, everybody else got their boats out of here this morning, and the coast guard told everyone to be off the water by sunset. I would have taken off earlier ... but I got held up."

As he spoke, a shot of wind screeched across from behind. Chills erupted down my arms, not from cold but from the unmistakable sense that danger was coming. Something in my core, something that couldn't be measured by the weather reports, knew the storm was quickly rolling against the horizon.

I pointed to my right. "I think there are a lot of sandbars over toward the mainland. I can see some of them."

"Yeah, I'm going to swing out wide and enter the river head-on so we don't get too close to the shallow spots. It's low tide, so it's harder than usual to get through."

We puttered into the dark expanse of the bay. As the water passed beneath us, the air grew wilder and burned my nostrils with sprays of salt. We were far from the island now, and far beyond us I could begin to make out the marshland that marked the river's entrance.

And then, without warning, the boat came to a stop.

We jolted forward and then back from the inertia. The engine wheezed until Josh cut the motor. I looked to him for explanation as he rushed to the rear to check the propellers. I followed, and we jutted our heads over the stern. There was nothing below us but the darkness of the water, but we could tell that the boat was not moving against the current. We had hit something, and the propellers of the boat were sunk into it like an anchor.

Josh rubbed his forehead. "We must've hit a sandbar."

"But we're nowhere near land!" I scanned the water around us. Flat and smooth. "There is nothing popping above the water. I didn't see anything."

"Missy, it's not your fault. I don't have the right lights on this thing. This sandbar's got to be at least a few feet below the surface." He started the engine again, this time moving the lever to reverse. It wheezed, but it didn't move. He cut the motor off and spoke calmly. There was no anger in his eyes anymore, only focus. "I'm gonna need to get in and dig it out."

"Dig it out? Josh, we're in the middle of the water, and it's after dark. You know what's in there at night, and you don't even know that we actually hit a sandbar. For all you know, we hit One-Eyed Willie down there."

A short chuckle escaped his lungs, and I let the corners of my lips come up in a small smile.

He shook off my comment, removed his shirt and shoes, and jumped into the black bay beneath. I had expected him to land waist deep, but he submerged completely and didn't surface for another two seconds. Just feet away from our engine, the water was far over his head.

The sandbars were impossible to predict: Shallow. Deep. Shallow. If we had steered just a few feet to the left, we wouldn't have hit the bar.

Josh's head bobbed in the water until he made his way to the engine and stood on the sand. He ducked beneath the surface and appeared again — over and over — doing his best to maneuver the sand and seaweed from around the engine. But he came up with nothing. It seemed the full weight of the boat had slammed the propellers into the bar with such force that the blades were buried to their necks. Finally, he submerged for a full minute before popping up and gasping for air.

"I'm getting in too. I can help."

"No, Melissa. There's no sense in that. It's not working. And we need a spotter."

I was not going to be a spotter when he needed help digging. I plunged into the water and made my way to his side. Below the surface, I clawed at the sand that was suffocating the metal blades. We dove down together and pulled at the propeller, but no amount of effort seemed to help. We didn't make a dent. The propellers were locked in, sucked in, and unmovable beneath the awesome weight of the wooden boat.

Josh spit salt water from his mouth. "We can't get it out like this, and the boat is too heavy to shake it free. Half of the belly is probably fixed into the bank." He tugged on the top of the engine to demonstrate. "Nothing we do is going to be enough. And we can't wait for high tide to raise us off the bank. The storm could be here by then, and there's no guarantee that the engine hasn't been damaged." His mouth shut at perfect rest. He wasn't going to say anything else. I sat in my own silence as he held the side of the ladder steady for me to climb up.

A torrent of water plummeted from my shorts to the steps below as I rose from the bay. By the time we settled on to the deck, the breeze had kicked up enough to make the summer water feel cold against our bodies.

He raised an eyebrow. "So, this is the one time in your life that you're not wearing a bathing suit, huh? I'm sorry I don't have a towel on board."

He handed me his gray jersey T-shirt, and I slipped it on over my wet top. I pulled my shirt off from underneath, threading it through the neck hole of his like a magician. He forced a smile to show me he was impressed.

"If you get me out of here, I'll show you how it's done."

His eyes hit the deck. He wasn't laughing anymore.

I took a seat opposite him. "Well, I guess we need to call somebody. It's gonna take them awhile to get out here, and who knows what other calls they're getting."

Josh didn't move, except to stare down at his phone.

"Don't you want to make a call now?"

He lifted up his cell phone to show me the error message. "There's no reception out here on the water. I can't even send a text." He swallowed hard.

I shrugged. "Okay, well, the boat must have a radio, right?"

He shook his head slightly. "No."

"You can't mean ..."

"There's no way to call for help."

I looked across the horizon. The Sunshine Skyway Bridge glowed miles away to the north. To our west, toward the overwhelmingly large expanse in that direction, the dark hand of the Gulf of Mexico had extended its fingers into the bay and into the currents drifting around our boat. If we were on land, we could have walked the few miles to the closest house, or even to our own homes. But on water, the distance may as well have been a hundred miles. I held my words as a small rush of panic began to settle in. Being run aground on a normal night might be an adventure. But being stranded in the dark when a hurricane was set to arrive and every boat had long since tied up was madness.

"I'm sure there's a way to call for help, Josh. Maybe there's something under these seat cushions."

"There's not." He looked to his feet. He didn't even move to search.

"Or some flares, even. How do you know? It's the pastor's boat. He's got to have something under here."

"Trust me on this."

I couldn't. I began to pull up the tops of the seats to search through the storage bins below. There was nothing inside any of them. We were sailing in a hollowed-out log, as if it hadn't been out to sea in years. "There's not even a life jacket under these seats!"

Josh rubbed the back of his neck. "I'm so sorry. This boat wasn't supposed to go in the water yet. I was only moving it because of the storm. I didn't think for a second that we'd have problems just taking it up the river. I wasn't even planning on driving it this far into the bay."

"How could it not have any life jackets?" I paced the boat in a fury, unable to concentrate on Josh's words. "What kind of pastor doesn't put life jackets on a family boat? Isn't he supposed to be all about following the rules?"

"It doesn't matter now. We have to deal with what we've got."

"It does matter, Josh. Look at us. We're out here in the middle of nowhere. Land isn't even in sight."

He leaned over and rested his elbows on his knees. "Land is in sight, Melissa."

I looked to the horizon in confusion. The closest land was the dim marsh of the preserve at the mouth of the river, over a mile away, at least. "Yeah, well, it may as well be in Timbuktu."

"It's close enough."

I crossed my arms as fear poured into the space between my bones and into the muscles of my neck and lips. "Josh, you're not thinking we could swim it?"

"No," he answered. "Not *we*."

"You can't be serious. It's almost pitch black out now. And you know what they catch out here at night, and you know about these currents. There's no way anyone could swim that far."

"Missy, we can't be here when the storm surge comes. And we've got next to no time before the rain begins and the winds kick up. There's no other option."

"Another boat will come by. Let's just wait. I'm sure someone will show up."

His eyes scoured the bay around us. "Any other night, and we could count on another boat to come by. But no one's out tonight."

"Josh, we don't even have a life jacket, and you're talking about making a swim that's got to be impossible on a good day."

I could see his lips tighten as he planned. He wasn't asking for my permission. He was telling me how it was going to be. He nodded if only to placate me. "I'll give it a few minutes. That's it."

I took a seat on the wood bench beside him. Our arms brushed one another in the cramped space. The moon peeked between a break in the clouds, and I could see the water looked to be smooth as steel, just like the time I had imagined swimming across it into infinity. Except now, instead of fantasizing about escaping into the Gulf, I wanted nothing more than to be back on the island, no matter how miserable I had believed myself to be there. Nowhere, it seemed, could offer me shelter or peace.

Josh stared straight ahead at the marsh as it loomed on the horizon like a dark shadow. He spoke quietly, evenly. "Even if we see a boat, there's no guarantee it will see us. We don't have flares. We don't have an air horn. And the spotlight on the bow is so small, it's practically invisible."

"Just wait. Please. I'm sure someone will come by." I couldn't face what I knew was coming. "I hate boats. I hate boats so much."

Josh looked to the deck, unwilling to respond.

"What's so special about this old boat, anyway? If Bill knew we were out here in this thing, he'd have a fit. What kind of pastor would ask you to take care of an old pile of wood like this when there's a category two storm on its way?"

"Does it matter?"

"Yes!" I pounded the bench with my fist. "He's supposed to be concerned about you, not his boat. But instead he asks you to take a boat with no safety equipment up the river."

Josh bounced his knee in nervous energy. "No, he didn't."

"What?"

"He doesn't even know."

I turned to Josh in shock. "Then why would you bother? Why are we even out here?"

Josh grew silent, frozen, as if he was afraid to look me in the eyes.

Something wasn't right. I rose from the bench and surveyed the deck, the captain's chair, the door to the small cabin. It all looked so familiar. It was an old fishing boat, the kind they use in Cortez Village, a kind I see all the time. But this boat looked ...

"Josh."

"Missy, don't ..."

The boat was white now. Painted, all barnacles removed. But it was the same, the very same. I stepped closer, towering over him as he kept his eyes on the deck. "Why do you care so much about this boat?"

Josh swallowed hard, his eyes glassed over with liquid as he finally looked toward me.

"Robby?" I turned to the wooden rail and ran my fingers along its side, and felt the wood beneath my feet. It was my brother's boat. It was the one he had worked so hard to recover, to repair. It was the one Bruce stole from under his hands because of what my mother had done. It was the only thing that he had ever taken hope in, and it was worthless.

Josh choked back the hoarseness in his voice. "I haven't been working extra hours at the store. I bought this after the funeral—Bruce gave me a deal to take it off his hands. I've been trying to finish it."

"What? Why?" I gripped the railing.

"This was Robby's dream. I wanted to make it right."

"Make it right?" I felt my chest pull together like a fist. "This boat destroyed him."

"It has nothing to do with why he's gone, Missy."

"How can you say that? I lost my brother because of this boat!" I charged to Josh's side, and felt my fists pound against the wood behind him.

He looked up with fierceness in his eyes. "I lost Robby too. But this boat isn't why. You just want to point to it in order to make some sense of all this. But it's not why he's gone."

"Robby's gone because he was chasing after some stupid idea of how this boat was going to fix everything. And I know it was never going to fix everything. But if Bruce hadn't taken it from him ..."

"No, Missy." He rubbed the side of his cheeks, as if he was turning the dials of a dam. When his mouth opened to speak, it was as if a levy had finally given way. "The fact is we're never going to fully know why Robby isn't here. It's bigger than us. And we can look at Bruce, or this boat, or the drugs, or even if he was horribly depressed, and try to make sense of it. But in the end, it will never make sense to us because it never should have happened. But I do know this—Robby never knew what he was worth. And that to me was bigger than whatever happened with this boat. And what scares me the most is that I don't think you're any different. Robby chased after the boat. What were you chasing after to fix everything? Approval? Some moment when everybody sees you and finally likes you? Everyone finally loves you because you're just like them, and then what?"

I felt my spine lose its strength and took a seat on the bench across from him. "It's easy for you to say, Josh. You don't know what it's like to have everyone look at you like ... Or to come from the kind of family I come from. Or know that I can't even be like those girls at church who have everything together."

He leaned forward with his hands folded and refused to look away from my eyes. "You're still expecting to fight their way and win. Your mom is the same way. Still looking for some fix, or someone or something that gets you out. But nothing you're looking at has any hope of saving any of you — not the way you really need. No boat. No guy ... Not even Sam."

"Sam?"

Josh settled against the back of the bench. Spent, expressionless.

"What about Sam?"

He turned his head from me.

The moon slipped behind the cloud covering again and a deeper shade of night settled over our faces. We could no longer see the edge of the horizon. We could no longer make out the difference between the sky and water that was lying beyond the boat. The marsh ahead had been erased from our sight.

Josh cleared his throat, and with it a catch of emotion. "I know about your hookup on the beach. I saw it myself."

A blush swept over my cheeks, and I could see my mistake blazing its way across Josh's face. I pulled my hands to the back of my neck, but I couldn't hide. I couldn't undo the fact that I had kissed Sam.

Josh shook his head in defeat.

I couldn't be losing him, not him too. Even if Josh didn't want me as a girlfriend, I couldn't lose his friendship.

"What was I supposed to do, Josh? You didn't want me. You made that clear. I heard about you hanging out with Jenny that night. I'm not good enough for you."

"That's what you heard, huh?"

"I'm not like her. I tried. And I couldn't be like her — like any of the other girls. I can't escape what I am."

"And what is that?"

I shook my head in disgust. Was he going to make me say it? My eyes filled with tears. Anger burned within my belly and my cheeks grew hot underneath my wet hair. "Look at what I did to Robby.

I turned my back when he needed me. Look at who my mother is. Even you said I'm the same as her. All those girls around you are going to grow up and marry someone like you and be respectable, and I'll always be on the outside of a life like that. I'm no good, and I don't deserve any better. I'm that tainted glass Pastor Bill was talking about, and there's no way for me to go back."

Josh stood up and leaned against the console, tense from the adrenaline that was surely pumping through his veins. "Melissa, the only difference between them and you is that they know they've been forgiven. Those moments you regret not going back to Robby, and every other thing you've done that you wish you could take back or undo, they need to be put to death. Jesus died and rose again to set you free from all of that. You missed that part of the story because your guilt wouldn't let you hear it. You thought you had to carry this on your own, but Jesus can take them to the cross for you. And that burden you carry is the only real difference between the girls at church and you.

"And, no, I'm not dating Jenny. She's been my friend since I was a kid. I didn't push you away because you're not good. I ran away because I thought you chose Sam all over again."

I looked at the boat, a heap of junk bobbing in the water that he had spent all summer repairing, just like he had spent all summer trying to repair me. "I guess I don't understand you, Josh. I don't understand what it is you want."

He moved across the deck to sit beside me. The anger was gone from his dark eyes, and his arm moved behind my shoulders. "You don't understand me because I haven't had the courage to tell you. I've done everything but say it. Melissa, I've wanted to be with you since the day I saw you. And when Sam stepped in, I stayed on the sidelines because I thought that's what a good friend needed to do. I could tell he was the one you were after. I tried to hide how I felt. I protected you from Sam because that was easier for me. But I was protecting myself too. I didn't think I had what it took when you had a world of guys knocking down your door. And what I wanted most of all is for you to know how amazing you are. How amazing I think you are."

"So why didn't you ever tell me?" I turned to meet his eyes.

He exhaled. "I guess I didn't have the faith. To fight."

"So, no Jenny?"

"No Jenny."

"And this boat?"

Josh smiled. "I wanted to show you there's a reason for hope, even in all of this. To show myself the same thing, maybe. To show you how I feel about you — that you're beautiful in every way."

"Beautiful? I've never felt like that. Not ever."

"Melissa, you can spend your life like everyone else — chasing what you think will make you better. Or you can let God show you how amazing you already are. I've been trying to show you that, and I've just been getting in the way. But I can promise you, he's even more in love with you than I am."

My breath abandoned my lungs. In love?

"This whole time, Melissa, I have just been trying to show you how I see you."

I could see it all now. Josh was always there, waiting for me to see him. But my sights were always somewhere else. "And I was focused on Sam. You lost a friendship over all this, didn't you? Trying to protect me? He couldn't stand it."

Josh swallowed. My quiet next-door neighbor had already said enough.

"Sam did kiss me on the beach. And I kissed him back, at first. But there on the beach I decided I would rather be faithful to the hope of you than be with him."

"If I had fought for you, you wouldn't have been left to wonder how I feel. I'm going to fight now, though."

Josh took my hand in his and pulled it to his mouth. He pressed his lips against the top of my folded fingers and shut his eyes. His lips moved slightly, and I could tell he was praying.

By the time he jumped into the water, I had already lost sight of him.

Chapter 19

People never ask me the right question when they ask me what happened at the beginning of my senior year. They always ask what his last words were. They figure he would have had great ones, the kind that would haunt a girl and echo off of empty lockers long after graduation. They wait breathlessly for me to describe the moment he jumped off the boat and into the glass-topped Gulf, cutting the ribbon of moonlight on the surface with the white of his arms.

But I never saw Josh swim away because he didn't want me to find him. He must have known that I would have jumped in after him, and that would have only put myself at risk. I waited with my hands on the rim of the boat, desperate to hear a splash or to see a movement, but nothing showed itself in the darkness.

If I jumped in, maybe I could catch up to him or maybe he would hear me and turn back. There was no way he could make it to shore. Even if the things lurking under the water left him alone, I was sure the tide would not. There was no way he could possibly hope to fight the current.

I stood on the edge of the deck with my bare toes wrapped around the wood beneath. There wasn't another vessel in sight. There wasn't a sound but the wind that began to push in from the east. We were alone.

No, now I was alone.

I jumped into the water and hoped the sound of the splash would shock Josh out of his mission. I surfaced with a mouth full of salt water and swam fifteen feet out until I felt the absence of the boat behind me. If Josh had heard me, he didn't turn around. And I could see no sign of him, not even a ripple.

I treaded water until a swell came over top of me and pushed me under. The ocean was deep beneath me, and I wondered how far it plunged below. When I resurfaced, I coughed up another mouthful of salt water and could see the first drops of rain smack the surface. For all the night swimming I did in all my efforts to escape the island, I knew I still wasn't strong enough to make it to shore on my own. I surrendered and made my way back to the boat. When I finally arrived on the deck, I scoured the horizon for any sign of Josh. In the far distance behind me, lights from the island flickered as trees flashed in front of their beams. The storm was beginning to stir, and he was nowhere in sight.

The water began to turn as the wind started to blow more steadily. The arrival of Hurricane Paul was subtle, but it was the beginning of the beast. The lion was stirring from his den, and I could feel the vessel leaning away from the edge of the bay and toward the dark, magnetic waters of the deep.

I sheltered myself beneath the ledge of the captain's console. If I crawled inside the cubby beneath it, I could escape the rain for as long as it was just a drizzle but still keep watch for any help. I tucked my knees into my chin and imagined every wave that was trying to topple Josh in his path. He wasn't only fighting the current now. He was fighting swells that were growing larger by the minute. He needed rescue. The storm opened and the tide began to rise with a quickness. Lightning illuminated the sky far away.

I couldn't lose him. I couldn't lose him too. He needed a miracle. And I had no right to ask for one. "I'm scared. Please, don't take him." The words left my mouth before I remember deciding to speak them.

Josh couldn't possibly be stronger than the river current that was pushing its force out to sea. I had no control. I had no way to fix it. Again. The mere thought moved me to my knees.

"God."

The word startled me. I had said it countless times before but this time I was calling a name. I was calling him. "If you are out there, and you can hear me, please let Josh be safe. Please, get him to shore. I know I don't deserve to ask you for anything—I've messed up too many times. I let Robby down when he needed me. I ran around using people, and I let them use me. I can't go on like this. And I can't fix this situation I'm in now. I want what Josh says you can offer. Please forgive me and take away this weight, this poison, in my life. And give me the strength to forgive others who failed my brother. I need you now." The wind picked up. "And I need your help."

Josh had said the only difference between the church girls and me was that they had been forgiven. Even after I'd asked for it, it felt too easy, too convenient. A prayer, a faith that gave them some relationship with God, a God who is invisible to everyone else? But had any of them turned their back on their brother when he needed them? Did any of them have to travel that far?

But Josh knew everything about me, and he still stayed close. And now he was risking his life to save mine. I didn't deserve a friend like this, who loved me for no reason—who loved me despite my mistakes.

I caught my breath as the thought entered my mind. Could God love me this way too? If Josh was going to jump off this boat and trust in God to save us, couldn't I trust him as well?

My eyes filled with tears when I opened them, and I half expected the sea to swallow me whole right there. And then the rain broke, and a cloud moved. The moon shone on me and lit the boat with a soft spotlight glow. It was enchanting, as if for just a moment there wasn't a storm lurking over the edge of the sea.

"Is that you?" I asked breathlessly.

The drenched boat's planks glistened under the brief shimmer of light. Across from me, on a board just inches away from where I sat, I saw an image carved into the dark-brown grooves. Discretely placed, right below the captain's wheel, I could make it out clearly in the moonlight:

R̃K

It was my brother's signature.

I crawled to touch it and ran my fingers over the carving. Something inside the ridges gave it a white gleam. The white was smooth and fragile. I examined it closer.

Doves.

Numerous doves from Crystal's sand dollars wedged into place, in the lines of my brother's letters.

I remembered Crystal's words to my brother. "Now you can always remember this moment. Peace!"

He had placed them in his name on this boat. And I could see it now. There, in the old wood, cemented into my brother's name by his own hands. Peace.

"God, you knew this was going to happen, didn't you?"

Tears ran down my face, but I couldn't contain my smile. I had figured my brother's dream had died with him, and I had pictured his boat rotting away in an old marina. And yet the very thing I'd blamed for ruining my brother, the thing that had shipwrecked me in a storm beyond my control, had brought me to the place where I discovered the giver of real, perfect peace. And no one was here to see this awesome thing but me. For the first time in my life, I truly felt beautiful.

• • • • •

When the sheriff pulled his boat next to mine, he spoke the first words I had heard since Josh told me he loved me. "It's okay. We're here."

When I climbed aboard the deck of his boat, Josh was waiting, wrapped in a blanket. "I made it," he whispered.

Relief swept over my body. I ran to him and flung my arms around his neck. "I prayed you would."

His hug increased at my words. He pulled me inside the cabin, out of the rain, as the sheriff rounded our stranded vessel and turned back toward the island.

Josh grasped my hand and pointed out the window toward Robby's boat. "They don't have enough time to save it."

I looked at the place where my brother had pinned his dreams, where he had carved his name. He had spent himself on that vessel because it was the only place he had found hope. He had dreamed it would be the way to get us out of the life we knew.

"We can let it go," I said. "It's done its job." I grieved my brother again in that moment, but this time I didn't feel I was grieving alone. I felt I was in the cup of hands greater than myself. This time I had a hope that neither of us would ever feel alone again.

Josh brushed my wet hair away from my cheek and lifted my chin until my eyes met his.

A small grin forced itself across his lips. He took my hand and kissed it. This time it wasn't a kiss good-bye. He looked at me with his eyes as dark as the sea, and I tried not to blink. I did not want to miss a second of Josh Durham holding me.

I didn't want to miss another second of that night, when I knew heaven and earth had been moved because a Father loved me. And the evidence was staring back at me; the greatest friend I had ever had, who had dared to love me with a love that was bigger than either of us. For the first time in my life, conviction filled up the still waters of my soul, moonlit, it seemed, by the revolutionary love I never knew I had. And it was growing brighter, toward the dawn, with every moment. We waited for the great and wonderful tide to come in, and trusted that it would be good.

Acknowledgments

Thank you, Jesus, for showing me that none of it was wasted. All praise, honor, and glory to You. This is my first book, and for that I owe more gratitude than I can express. Thank you, my gifted and brave brother Ryan Quigley (TBBITW, which I think says it all, really). Thank you, Quigley and Burke clans, for your love and support (most dearly Nanny Joan Burke and Aunt Debby Bedell for the countless mercies that led to this piece). Thank you, Kimberly Caldwell and Monica Enfield, my constant anchors, inspiration, and best friends. Thank you, Cupcakes for Christ small group, who for eight years and going have been my sisters, especially Elizabeth Podgorski and Anne Brubaker for walking every step of the way with me, Jessica Neff for inspiring me, Julie Stanos, Anna Szeto, Toni Randolph, Stephanie Lin, and Amanda Roberts for blessing me with your gifts and trust, the many other members whose love I cherish, and Leslie Ryser for starting it all and eating sugar. Thank you, great friends and teachers who have dreamed with me for so many years: dear sister Launa Stewart who, among other things, helped me take the big leap; Kristine Hopkins; Erika Smakula; Michelle Whittaker; incredible mentor and friend José Cunningham, Jessica O'Neil, and the amazing team at Crowell & Moring LLP; Scott Sobel for teaching me about stories and believing in mine; Tom Newman of Impact Productions; Dr. Janice Pope of Appalachian State University; Jon Scott of Manatee High School; Anita Brendle of Pine Castle Elementary; and former Manatee AM editor Bruce Kestin, rest in peace. Thank you, Jim Nelson, Susan McSwain, and all others who poured into me through YoungLife when I was a teenager, as well as Gregory McKee and the staff at YMCA Camp Greenville. You changed my life forever. Thank you to ACFW for showing me it's possible. Thank you, editor extraordinaire, Jacque Alberta of Zondervan. You believed in my work and made it better. Thank you to the entire team at Zondervan and Zonderkidz, including marketing guru Sara Merritt. Thank you, Capital Life Church (Pastor Bill and Lisa Shuler), McLean Bible, and Janet Raymond for teaching me the ways of Christ. I am still learning. Thank you, critique partners Connie Almony and Courtney Linville. Thank you, agent Leslie Stobbe. Thank you, great people of Anna Maria Island and Bradenton, FL, who know exactly how special our home is. And thank you, Poppo and Gram. I can't wait to see what you have to say about all of this one day.

Like Moonlight at Low Tide addresses two serious issues that impact many during our teen years and beyond: the effects of bullying and suicide. No fiction book can explore all of the emotional, physical, and spiritual aspects of these two struggles. So if you or someone you know is struggling with suicidal thoughts, please call 911 (or your local emergency authorities) or reach out to a trusted adult immediately. If you're struggling with issues of self-worth, Christian churches and organizations such as YoungLife, as well as school counselors, can also provide support and the voice of truth you deserve. If you're reading this, know you have a purpose in your life that is good. It is never too late to ask for help or for a fresh start. You can also find resources through the American Association of Christian Counselors at www.aacc.net or 1-800-526-8673.

Reading Guide

Share your answers on Nicole Quigley's author page at: *www.facebook.com/nicolequigleybooks*

1. The things we want the most often reveal the unspoken questions we ask ourselves. What questions do you think Melissa is asking of herself when we meet her at the beginning of the book?

2. When Melissa returns to the island after having been away for a few years, she struggles with the memory of how things once were, and worries about how things might be again. Have you ever felt the same way? Do you think Missy's feelings are based on things from the past or things that are happening in the present?

3. Once Melissa returns to school, she sees her longtime crush, Sam King, as well as her former bullies. If she could wish for three things at that moment, what do you think they would be? Why?

4. One of Melissa's hopes is to be told she is beautiful so that she will never be known as "Messy" again. What are some things you deeply want to hear, and who has the power to say them to you?

5. Denise's mood changes drastically when Bruce Paczkowski enters the scene. What does this say about Denise's greatest desires?

6. At one point Missy notes her laugh around Sam when they're flirting heavily is a lot like her mom's laugh around the men in her life. How much is Missy following Denise's pattern? How is she different from her mother?

7. Rebellion is defined as acting in opposition against something that can influence our thoughts, opinions, or behavior. Why does Melissa think Josh's Bible reading shows he is in the middle of a personal rebellion? What are the consequences of his rebellion throughout this story?

8. The first time Melissa speaks about the Christian faith and the Bible, she declares there is no way to know if it is true and says that people have corrupted it. What work or research has she done to make this claim? Have you ever heard people say the same thing as Missy? Have you even thought it yourself at some point?

9. Which of Melissa's personal experiences might have influenced her to believe that she couldn't be forgiven, or be like the girls who goes to Josh's church? How might Missy's story have been different if she had let go of her personal misconceptions sooner?

10. Melissa feels that becoming a Christian would be "too convenient" and too easy to erase the regret she carries. Have you ever felt like you could never be good or pure enough? How did you deal with those feelings?

11. At the end of the story, Sam wants to start a new relationship with Missy. Do you think he has changed at all by the end of the summer? Why do you think he wants Missy back?

12. Melissa finally feels joy and transformation in the last scene, although she is still suffering from grief. What realizations have brought her hope even though she still deeply grieves for her brother? How do you think Missy's story continues beyond the last paragraph of the book?

Interrupted

A Life Beyond Words

Rachel Coker

Can love really heal all things?

If Sam Carroll hadn't shown up, she might have been able to get to her mother in time. Instead, Allie Everly finds herself at a funeral, mourning the loss of her beloved mother. She is dealt another blow when, a few hours later, she is sent from Tennessee to Maine to become the daughter of Miss Beatrice Lovell, a prim woman with a faith Allie cannot accept.

Poetry and letters written to her mother become the only things keeping Allie's heart from hardening completely. But then Sam arrives for the summer, and with him comes many confusing emotions, both toward him and the people around her. As World War II looms, Allie will be forced to decide whether hanging on to the past is worth losing her chance to be loved.

"Sweeping epic" –Booklist

"A feel-good story for both heart and soul." –Kirkus Reviews

"An impressive debut." –Publishers Weekly

Available in stores and online!

Chasing Jupiter

Rachel Coker

Scarlett Blaine's life in 1960s Georgia isn't always easy, especially given her parents' financial struggles and the fights surrounding her sister Juli's hippie lifestyle. Then there's her brother, Cliff. While Scarlett loves him more than anything, there's no denying his unique behavior leaves Cliff misunderstood and left out. So when he wishes for a rocket to Jupiter, Scarlett agrees to make it happen, no matter how crazy the idea might be.

Raising the rocket money means baking pies, and the farmer's son, Frank, agrees to provide the peaches if Scarlett will help him talk to Juli. The problem is, Scarlett really enjoys her time with Frank, and finds herself wondering if, someday, they could be more than friends. Just as she thinks everything might be going her way, Cliff suffers an accident that not only affects the rocket plans, but shakes Scarlett's view of God. As the summer comes to an end, Scarlett must find a way to regain what she's lost, but also fulfill a promise to launch her brother's dream.

Available in stores and online!